A SUMMARY OF BANKRUPTCY LAW

M. JONATHAN HAYES

M. Jonathan Hayes
Certified Bankruptcy Specialist
jhayes@polarisnet.net
9700 Reseda Blvd., Suite 201
Northridge, CA 91324

www.lawprofessorblogs.com

www.hayesbklaw.com

Table of Contents

INTRODUCTION

Bankruptcy pundits like to point out that bankruptcy has been around since the time of the bible. Deuteronomy 15:1says: "At the end of every seven years you shall grant a release of debts. And this is the form of the release: Every creditor who has lent anything to his neighbor shall release it; he shall not require it of his neighbor or his brother, because it is called the Lord's release."

That is a fun sort of thought but bankruptcy, until fairly recently, has never been about the discharge of debts. The purpose of bankruptcy has always been, and indeed was invented, to help creditors seize and sell the debtor's assets in the most efficient manner. By requiring creditors to act as a group, the debtor's assets can be sold for the highest value and distributed fairly to all creditors pro-rata. The first discharge came in England in 1705, Statute of 4 Anne. Under that law, a debtor who was insolvent and cooperated with the location and distribution of his assets to his creditors received a discharge and 5% of the assets. Debtors who did not meet with their creditors, who lied to them, or who refused to reveal the whereabouts of all of their assets were *hanged*. There was no such thing as an automatic discharge of debts in America until the turn of the century, the Bankruptcy Act of 1898. Indeed, the discharge provided in early American bankruptcy and state insolvency laws permitted the cooperative debtor to be discharged *from jail* when his assets were sold and distributed to creditors. He received a discharge of debts, if at all, only upon distribution of a specified return to creditors and a positive vote of a specified number of creditors.

Today the focus of bankruptcy, at least at the level of the individual, is the discharge of debts which is automatic with a few exceptions. While it is automatic however, it is not a constitutional right. The Supreme Court said so in *United States v Kras*,[1] five to four, that it was not a denial of due process to require the payment of a filing fee before allowing a petition to be filed. Nor is there any right to a "fresh start." Those words are not in the bankruptcy code. In fact, a national bankruptcy law existed for only about 15 years of the first 110 odd years of our country. Congress today could abolish bankruptcy completely if it wanted, or abolish

---

[1] 409 U.S. 434 (1973)

chapter 7 leaving chapter 13, or abolish the discharge (and I suspect that has been suggested to Congress by the credit card industry lately).

Nearly all individuals today who file chapter 7 do so for the discharge. They have no assets to "maximize" – to seize and sell and distribute to creditors pro-rata, nothing creditors would get outside of bankruptcy anyway. The chapter 7 is typically a bunch of forms, of growing complexity unfortunately, and a five minute meeting with the trustee. No one objects to the discharge so it is entered by the clerk when the objection period runs. It is a rare chapter 7 when the debtor meets the judge assigned to the case.

Persons interested in filing bankruptcy are typically consumed with telling me about their creditors; which one is impossible to deal with, which one will probably take half, etc. They want to tell me how they got into the current predicament, and whose fault it really is. They never expected or intended to "go bk." I try to act interested but I am getting old. I focus on assets – what do they have that they will lose, that the trustee will sell? It often takes a while to drag that information out of the client. When the goal is to save an asset that they would otherwise lose, I focus on how much they will have to pay, in chapter 13 or chapter 11, to keep the asset. Sometimes the focus is on debts – which debts will survive the bankruptcy? They need to know that to make the decision on whether to file and which chapter to use.

Until 2009, I would have bet you that the overwhelming percentage of individuals who file chapter 7 do so to stop the credit card collection phone calls. They have run up more credit card debt than they can pay and are being threatened daily on the telephone. Sometimes they cannot pay the credit cards because of a loss of job or some other calamity, but just as often they simply got in over their head – the easy credit just snuck up on them. A chapter 7 case then is completely appropriate in my view. But recently I have been seeing a lot of individuals filing chapter 7 to discharge business debts, the guarantees they signed, the vendor that is suing them, or the landlord of the failed or failing business. More individuals than before have bought real property in the last few years in other states and are being threatened with deficiency claims. Many individuals took HELOCs which are being wiped out by the foreclosure of the senior lender and are filing chapter 7 to avoid the collection lawsuit.

About one-third of bankruptcy cases today are chapters 13s. This is the option created to help the debtor save her home. Mortgage defaults may be cured over time or re-written in some instances. The chapter 13 plan proposed by the debtor and approved by the court must pay home loans in full per the original terms and must pay creditors more than they would get in a chapter 7. If the debtor does not have sufficient income to make the required payments, chapter 13 will not work, the case will be dismissed.

Chapter 11 petitions, less than 1% of the total, range from mega cases General Motors, Chrysler and Lehman Bros to the small corporate or individually held business to Mr. and Mrs. Jones whose debts exceed the chapter 13 limits. Conceptually, chapter 11 cases and chapter 13 cases are very similar. The case is filed to save property from creditors. A plan is proposed which gives creditors the value of the property the debtor wants to keep. The mega cases tend to be about selling the assets in an organized manner or wiping out the shareholders giving new shares to creditors or new investors. The rest of the cases are about saving homes or small business assets.

In 2008, there were 1,097,000 bankruptcy petitions filed in the United States. Of these, 725,000 were chapter 7; 360,000 chapter 13; 10,000 chapter 11; 338 farmers filed chapter 12; 4 municipalities filed chapter 9; and there were 95 "international" chapter 15 petitions filed. Of the total, individuals filed 1,081,000 petitions and business entities filed about 16,000. Of the chapter 7 cases, about 96% - 97% were "no asset" meaning there were no non-exempt assets with equity for the trustee to sell. About 25% of chapter 13 cases are filed *in pro per* and virtually all are dismissed before any plan is confirmed.

Bankruptcy filings exceeded one million for the first time in 1996. The high for a single year before Congress passed the Bankruptcy Abuse Prevention and Consumer Protection Act ("BAPCPA") in 2005 was 1,660,000 in 2003, followed closely by 1,578,000 in 2004 and of the course the big hit, 2,078,000 in 2005. In 2005, when BAPCPA became effective, filings soared because of the belief that bankruptcy was suddenly going to disappear as an option for the beleaguered individual. Filings dropped to 615,000 in 2006 but are coming back. We expect about 1.5 million petitions in 2009.

BAPCPA is a disgrace in my opinion. It created numerous new hurdles for individuals, additional requirements and risk for attorneys, and significant confusion which has resulted in a two-fold increase in the cost of filing. The means test is a joke. Nearly everyone passes the means test filling out a form so complicated I could not fill it out myself without a bankruptcy forms computer program. Those who do not pass would have had their cases dismissed or converted under pre-BAPCPA law almost surely anyway. Congress has so far refused to fix even the most obvious errors in the amendments leaving it to individual courts and eventually courts of appeals to sort out - to try to guess what Congress meant and come up with a workable rule going forward.

Bankruptcy is thought to be a highly complex and confusing subject. But this is a bad rap in my view. In bankruptcy debtors lose only the assets they would have lost anyway. There are exceptions to be sure. Secured creditors in bankruptcy wind up with their collateral or the value of the collateral, same as outside of bankruptcy. Unsecured creditors get what's left, if anything, or the value of what's left. Bankruptcy practice does however involve a thorough knowledge of many diverse state and federal laws. The rights and duties of creditors, vendors, bailees, customers, spouses, heirs, transferees, holders-in-due course, purchasers, veterans, guarantors, partners, agents, co-debtors, employees, landlords, assignees, etc., etc., are, for the most part, determined by state and federal law *independent* of the bankruptcy code. A good example of this is the common issue of determining what a person "owns," the extent of his rights in property, a question answered entirely by non-bankruptcy law. The bankruptcy code does not create rights in general. It should be thought of as a *vehicle* for accomplishing a specific purpose; that of dividing up the debtor's non-exempt assets in the most efficient manner among his creditors according to their pre-bankruptcy rights. Non-bankruptcy law determines what the debtor owns and what the debtors owes. The bankruptcy code determines *how* those assets are distributed.

This book is designed to give a *general overview* of bankruptcy to the law student, the new attorney or any person interested in the subject. There are many exceptions to every statement made, most of which are not discussed because of my desire to keep the book basic and for beginners. The non-bankruptcy attorney reader of this book especially should not make decisions without consulting a competent attorney. I have set out only a few quotes directly from the statute. Read the code section cited. Read the Bankruptcy Rules cited and the state statutes cited. The words written in the code and rules are important; they are the same words the judge will be reading and enforcing; and the trustee, and your opponent. The code is easily twice as long as this book so there is a whole lot in the code which is not in this book.

Most of the cites in this book are Supreme Court cases or 9th Circuit cases. The 9th Circuit includes California where I live and work and frankly I have a hard enough time remembering what the law is here much less what it is somewhere else. Where state law is important, such as exemptions and rights of secured creditors, I cite California law for the same reason.

The Rutter Group book on Bankruptcy by Judges Alan Ahart and Leslie Tchaikovsky, and retired Judge Kathleen March is a great reference and resource. It is also geared to the world of California bankruptcy. In the chapter 13 arena, Judge Keith Lundin's book, Chapter 13, 3rd.Ed, is a must for your bookshelf. And by the way, if you ever get a chance to listen to Judge Lundin, don't miss the opportunity. He is an engaging and funny populist who has sat on the bankruptcy court in Nashville, Tennessee for many years. Every bankruptcy attorney in the Ninth Circuit should have a copy of Judge Randall Newsome's Research Notebook – print it out and keep it by your desk. You can get it online by doing a google search.

Many people helped me with this book. My friend, Peter Lively, one of the smartest bankruptcy lawyers I know, spent his valuable time in these busy days for bankruptcy attorneys reading this manuscript and giving me comments. Chapter 13 trustee Nancy Curry made numerous helpful comments on the chapter 13 section as did Judge Victoria Kaufman and my friend and confidant, Jim King. Dennis McGoldrick, a former chapter 7 trustee and great consumer bankruptcy attorney gave me advice and support. My wife, Gerry, always patient with me, read it and asked me many questions. Thanks.

M. Jonathan Hayes
Northridge, California
July, 2009

A Summary of Bankruptcy Law

PART ONE   OVERVIEW

A Summary of Bankruptcy Law

1. THE PLAYERS

1. The Debtor

The debtor is the person or entity who files a bankruptcy petition or against whom an involuntary petition is filed. Section 101(13)[2] When a husband and wife file together. They are known as joint debtors. Section 302

2. The Creditors

The creditors are the persons or entities to whom the debtor owes a debt. Section 101(10).   Creditors are said to have a "claim" against the debtor and are often called "claimants."

2.1 Secured Creditors.

Secured creditors are those who have a security interest in specific property of the debtor known as "collateral." The security interest, also known as a "lien," is usually created by contract between the debtor and the secured creditor, the "voluntary lien," but it also may be created by law such as an IRS lien or mechanics lien, the "involuntary lien."

2.2 Priority Creditors.

Priority creditors are *unsecured* creditors whose claims are paid before other *unsecured* creditors. Section 507. There are eight levels of priority creditors the most common being spousal and

---

[2] The current law of bankruptcy is found in Title 11 of the United States Code. It was enacted on November 6, 1978, as the Bankruptcy Reform Act of 1978, Pub. L. No. 95-598, 92 Stat. 2549 (effective October 1, 1979), and governs all cases filed on or after October 1, 1979. It has been amended several times, most comprehensively in 1984, 1986, 1994 and 2005. All references herein to "Section" are to this act.

child support, now known as "domestic support obligations," administrative expenses, certain wages and most taxes.

3. The Trustee

3.1 Chapter 7 Trustee

The chapter 7 trustee is a private individual, often a bankruptcy attorney, who is chosen by the United States Trustee's Office to administer the chapter 7 estate. His or her job is to maximize the assets of the estate and investigate the financial affairs of the debtor.[3] Section 704. He sells the assets, if there are any to be sold, and distributes the funds to the creditors. In the Central District of California, the U.S. Trustee's Office maintains a panel of approximately 40 trustees. The trustees in each particular case are chosen at random from this panel.

3.2 Chapter 13 Trustee

The chapter 13 trustee is an individual chosen by the U.S. Trustee to administer the chapter 13 estate. The chapter 13 trustee is a standing trustee meaning that the job is full time and permanent. The chapter 13 trustee's job is to investigate the financial affairs of the debtor and comment on the proposed chapter 13 plan. Section 1302 The trustee processes the monthly plan payments made by the debtor during the period the plan is in effect, usually three years to five years.[4]

3.3 Chapter 11 Trustee

The chapter 11 trustee is, at the outset of the chapter 11 case, the debtor himself (or itself). The debtor is known as the "debtor-in-possession" or "DIP." Section 1107 The debtor-in-possession has all of the rights and obligations of a chapter 7 trustee. Creditors may, however, ask the court to appoint an independent trustee during the case. Section 1104 If the court

---

[3] The chapter 7 trustee receives $65 per case, Section 330(b), from the filing fee plus a percentage of what he sells in the rare instance where there is something to sell. Section 326

[4] In the Central District of California there are five chapter 13 trustees. They will be assigned about 6,000 cases each in 2009.

grants the request, the trustee is chosen generally from the same panel as the chapter 7 trustees.

4. The United States Trustee's Office

The United States Trustee's Office ("UST") is a branch of the United States Department of Justice.[5] There are UST offices in every judicial district except Alabama and North Carolina. The UST was formed in 1979 to help the administration of the bankruptcy system. They appoint the various trustees, oversee the administration of cases, investigate fraud, and generally support the bankruptcy judges' activities. The Assistant United States Trustee in the Central District of California is Peter Anderson. He has approximately 20 attorneys on staff and about 60 employees in total. The U.S. Trustee has an excellent web site at www.usdoj.gov/ust.

5. The Judge

Bankruptcy Judges are federal judges appointed for a 14 year term.[6] There are 19 judges in the Central District of California. There are approximately 325 judges sitting in 94 judicial districts throughout the United States. Each bankruptcy case is assigned to a judge when the case is filed.

6. The Court

The Bankruptcy Court is a Federal Court. This is so because bankruptcy law is a federal law enacted by Congress under the power given to it by the United States Constitution. Article One, Section 8 entitled "Powers of Congress" provides that "Congress shall have Power . . . to establish uniform laws on the subject of bankruptcies." Congress created the Bankruptcy Court as a branch or an adjunct of the District Court in each of the federal districts throughout the United States.[7]   The Bankruptcy Court has jurisdiction over "all cases under title 11 and all core proceedings arising under title 11, or arising in a case under title 11."[8]

---

[5] See 28 U.S.C. 581
[6] 28 U.S.C. 152
[7] 28 U.S.C. 151; 28 U.S.C. 1334
[8] 28 U.S.C. 157

In the Central District of California there are five branches ("divisions") of the Bankruptcy Court: Los Angeles with 10 judges; Santa Ana with 3 judges; Riverside with 2 judges, San Fernando Valley with 3 judges and Santa Barbara with one judge.

All of the courts today have excellent web sites. The Central District of California site can be found at www.cacb.uscourts.gov.

2. OVERVIEW OF THE BASIC CHAPTERS

1.   Chapter 7

1.1 Who May File a Chapter 7?

A chapter 7 petition may be filed by any individual or entity, i.e., corporations, partnerships, business associations, except a railroad. Section 109(b). Banks and insurance companies may not file any bankruptcy chapter. Section 109(b)(2) The debtor need not be a resident of the United States. An individual whose debts are primarily consumer debts may file chapter 7 only if he passes the "means test" set forth in Section 707(b)(2) and the case is not otherwise an "abuse" of the bankruptcy process. Section 707(b)(3)

1.2 General

In a chapter 7, a trustee is appointed by the U.S. Trustee's Office immediately. His or her job is to seize and sell all of the assets owned by the debtor at the time of filing the petition which have equity and are not exempt. Section 704 At the same time, all debts owed by an individual at the time of filing with certain exceptions are instantaneously discharged. Section 727(b) Only individuals receive a discharge. Corporations, partnerships etc never receive a discharge of debts in chapter 7. Section 727(a)(1)

1.3 Advantages for the Debtor

The typical chapter 7 debtor has no assets that are subject to seizure by the trustee. In other words, all assets owned by the debtor at the time of filing are either exempt or have no equity.

These are called "no asset" cases. Therefore the advantage to the debtor is that he loses no assets but at the same time all of his debts, with the exceptions set forth in Section 523(a), are discharged.

2.   Chapter 13

2.1 Who May File a Chapter 13?

Only an individual with regular income may file a chapter 13 petition. The individual cannot have more than $1,010,650 in secured debts and $336,900 in unsecured debts.[9] Section 109(e) The debt limits apply to non-contingent, liquidated debts. Sec Section – below.

2.2 The Chapter 13 Plan

In a chapter 13, the individual proposes a plan to his or her creditors within 15 days after filing the petition. The plan must pay all of the net disposable income of the debtor over three to five years and that total amount must be more than creditors would receive in a chapter 7. Section 1325 The plan may cure defaults on home mortgages and other secured debts over three to five years. Creditors do not vote on the plan; if it meets the statutory requirements, it is confirmed by the court.

2.3 Chapter 13 Trustee

Chapter 13 trustees are full time standing trustees whose duties include reviewing and commenting on the chapter 13 plan proposed by the debtor. When the plan is confirmed by the court, the plan payments are made monthly to the trustee who then distributes the funds to the creditors. The trustee receives a percentage of the plan payment as compensation for the efforts.[10]

---

[9] These amounts are adjusted every three years. Section 104(b) The next adjustment will take place on April 1, 2010.
[10] In the Central District of California the percentage is 11%.

2.4 Advantages for the Debtor

In a chapter 13, the debtor loses no assets whatsoever. Section 1306 The debtors may use the plan to cure defaults on secured loans, the most common being home mortgages and automobile loans. Section 1322(b)   The debtor may also pay otherwise non-dischargeable debts such as student loans and taxes over a period of years.

2.5 The Chapter 13 Discharge

Upon completion of the Chapter 13 plan, the debtor receives a discharge of all debts existing on the petition date and not paid during the plan. Section 1328   In other words, if the plan pays creditors 20% of their claims over the course of the plan, the remainder is discharged upon completion of the payments.

3.   Chapter 11

3.1 Who May File a Chapter 11?

Any person or entity who qualifies to file a chapter 7 may file chapter 11 except stockbrokers. Section 109(d). There is no requirement that the debtor be engaged in a business or be insolvent. There is no means test in chapter 11 cases.

3.1.1 Individual Chapter 11 Cases

Often an individual will file a chapter 11 petition when he does not qualify for chapter 13 because of the debt limits in Section 109(e).

3.2 The chapter 11 Plan

A chapter 11 is similar in concept to chapter 13, that is, the debtor proposes a plan to its creditors. Section 1121   If the creditors vote for the plan, it is usually approved by the court. If the creditors vote against the plan, the court may still approve it over their objections.   That is commonly known as the "cramdown" powers of the court. Section 1129(b)

3.3 Advantages for the Debtor

The debtor stays in possession of its property and continues to operate its business. Section 1107 There is typically no trustee unless the court orders one, usually for gross mismanagement during the chapter 11 case. Section 1104 A chapter 11 plan has considerably more flexibility than a chapter 13 plan. Plan payments may be for many years for example.

3.4 Discharge

An individual chapter 11 debtor typically will receive a discharge of his debts when the chapter 11 plan is completed. Section 1141(d)(5) A corporate chapter 11 debtor will also receive a discharge of all debts provided that the plan is not a liquidation plan. Section 1141(d)(3)

4.   Chapter 9

Only a municipality may file a chapter 9 petition. Section 109(a). The debtor subsequently proposes a plan to its creditors similar in concept to a chapter 11 plan.

5.   Chapter 12

Only a farmer may file a chapter 12 petition. Section 109(f). The debtor subsequently proposes a plan to his creditors similar in concept to a chapter 13 plan.

6.   Chapter 15

Chapter 15 is entitled Ancillary and Other Cross-Border Cases. It was added to the code with the 2005 BAPCPA Amendments. It is commenced by the filing of a petition "for recognition of a foreign proceeding." Section 1504

7.   How Often May Bankruptcy be Filed?

There is no limit to how often a person may file a bankruptcy petition. A person may obtain a discharge of his debts in chapter 7 only once every eight years. Section 727(a)(8). Some debtors are not permitted to refile for six months after a previous case has been dismissed. Section 109(g)

3. COMMENCING THE BANKRUPTCY CASE

1.   Introduction

A bankruptcy case under every chapter is commenced by filing a "petition." Section 301   This is a three page form which has little more than the debtor's name, address, and which chapter the debtor is filing under. Along with the petition, there are a number of schedules which list the debtor's property, her debts, and claimed exemptions.[11]   These "schedules" include a statement of monthly income and expenses and a series of questions known as the "Statement of Financial Affairs." Section 521(a) The debtor must also file a "mailing matrix," a simple list of the name and address of every creditor. This is the list used by the clerk to give notice of the bankruptcy filing.

2. Venue

The bankruptcy petition is typically filed in the federal judicial district where the debtor has resided for the past six months or, if he has not resided in one district for the past six months, in the district where he has resided for the largest portion of the last six months. A bankruptcy petition may also be filed in the district where the debtor has its principle place of business or where the principle assets are located or where a related case is pending.[12]

3. Filing Fees

The filing fee for a chapter 7 case is $299; chapter 13 is $274; and, chapter 11 is $1,039 and must be paid with the petition. The filing fees may be paid in installments, and may be waived all together.[13]

---

[11] Rule 1007 (All cites in these footnotes to "Rule," are to the Federal Rules of Bankruptcy Procedure, effective December 1, 2008.
[12] 28 U.S.C. 1408, 1409
[13] Rule 1006

4.   Pre-Filing Credit Counseling

Individuals must complete a credit counseling program within 180 days prior to the bankruptcy filing before filing any bankruptcy case. The program must "outline the opportunities for available credit counseling and assist such individual in performing a related budget analysis." Section 109(h)(1) The credit counseling can be in a group, be individual, can be by telephone or through the internet. The various approved counseling agencies in each state can be found on the court's website or the U.S. Trustee's website.

4.1 Exceptions

1)   The US Trustee can make a determination that adequate counseling is not available in the district. Section 109(h)(2) That determination has not been made for any district in California.

2)   The debtor can submit a "certification" with his petition asking for a waiver of the requirement. The certification must a) "describe exigent circumstances," and, b) state that the debtor requested counseling but could not obtain the same within five days after the request, and c) be satisfactory to the court. After the filing, the debtor must obtain the counseling within 30 days (which can be increased by 15 days on approval of the court). Section 109(h)(3)

3) The debtor can ask the court for a waiver because of "incapacity, disability or active military duty in a military combat zone." Section 109(h)(4)

4.2 Effect of Non-Compliance on the Jurisdiction of the Court

In the 9th Circuit, the failure of the debtor to complete the credit counseling before filing his case does not affect the jurisdiction of the bankruptcy court.[14] The court may allow the case to proceed even though there was no compliance when the case was filed. Filing a petition without doing the counseling first

---

[14] *Mendez v. Salven (In re Mendez)*, 367 B.R. 109 (B.A.P. 9th Cir. 2009)(failure to do counseling does not relieve court of jurisdiction)

is playing with fire however. The code requires the counseling and it should not be ignored. If a case is filed without the counseling, for example, by a pro per or a lawyer with no brains, the non-complying debtor should do the counseling immediately after the filing and seek a court waiver of the prepetition failure.

4.3 The Certificate

The debtor must, with his petition, file a certificate from the credit counsel agency attesting that the debtor has received the required counseling and attach a copy of the "debt repayment plan, if any, . . . developed . . .through the agency."[15] Section 521(b)

4.4 The Details of Consumer Counseling

The U.S. Trustee's Office is charged with determining what entities will qualify to give the counseling required under the Act, how extensive the counseling will be, and how much the agency may charge. Section 111 The U.S. Trustee has promulgated applications and instructions to apply for certification as an approved Consumer Counseling Agencies. These can be found at www.usdoj.gov/ust/bapcpa/ccde.htm. The instructions suggest that the credit counseling briefing is expected to last 90 minutes.[16] The requirements appear to be pretty onerous with bonding requirements, quality control procedures and fairly qualified and trained counselors. The agency must agree to provide the counseling for free to people who cannot afford to pay any fee.

5. Disclosure of Paychecks

In addition to the petition and the schedules, the debtor must attach copies "of all payment advices or other evidence of payments received within 60 days before filing" from the debtor's employer. Section 521(a)(1)(B)(iv). If the debtor is self-employed or has not worked in the past 60 days, a statement must be filed attesting to that.

---

[15] I have not yet seen a "debt repayment plan" and understand that one is prepared only in rare instances.

[16] My understanding is that the counseling typically lasts 15 to 20 minutes, is completed on the telephone or on the internet, and is completely perfunctory.

6.   The Means Test Computations

An individual debtor must file a "statement of net monthly income itemized to show how the amount is calculated." Section 521(a)(1)(B)(v). This has come to be known as the Form B22 or the "means test." The means test is used primarily to determine whether the individual's chapter 7 petition is presumed to be an abuse of the bankruptcy process and therefore should be dismissed. In concept, individuals whose debts are primarily consumer debts and have the "means" to pay some meaningful portion of those debts presumptively do not qualify for chapter 7, i.e., the discharge.

7.   Emergency Filings

The debtor can file an emergency petition, sometimes known as a "face sheet" petition, by filing the petition and the creditors' mailing matrix only and paying the filing fee. The remainder of the schedules must be filed 15 days thereafter. The debtor can file a motion with the court asking for additional time beyond the 15 days if the debtor has a good reason for the extra time and files the motion with the court before the time elapses. The debtor must nevertheless complete the credit counseling before the filing.

4.   DUTIES OF DEBTOR'S COUNSEL SET FORTH IN THE BANKRUPTCY CODE

1. Attorney's "Certification" of the Accuracy of the Schedules

The Bankruptcy Code requires Debtor's counsel to "perform a reasonable investigation into the circumstances that gave rise to the petition and determine that the petition is well grounded in fact; and is warranted by existing law or a good faith argument for the extension, modification, or reversal of existing law and does not constitute an abuse." Section 707(b)(4)(C)

Debtor's counsel, by signing the petition, is certifying that he or she "has no knowledge after an inquiry that the information in the schedules filed with such petition is incorrect." Section 707(b)(4)(D)

2.   Debtor's Counsel as a "Debt Relief Agency"

The 2005 BAPCPA amendments added a new concept to the code - the "debt relief agency." A debt relief agency is defined as any "person who provides bankruptcy assistance to an assisted person in return for payment of money or other valuable consideration." Section 101(12A) An assisted person is defined as a person "whose debts consist primarily of consumer debts and the value of whose nonexempt assets are below $150,000." Section 101(3) While a number of different agencies are excluded, attorneys, in general, are not.[17] Therefore apparently an attorney giving bankruptcy advice for a fee to an "assisted person" is a debt relief agency and must meet the requirements of Sections 526, 527 and 528.

3.   Restrictions on Debt Relief Agencies

Generally a debt relief agency must provide good service to the "assisted person." Section 526 A debt relief agency shall not "advise an assisted person or prospective assisted person to incur more debt in contemplation of such person filing a case under this title or to pay an attorney or bankruptcy petition preparer fee or charge for services performed as part of preparing for or representing a debtor in a case under this title." Section 526(a)(4)

3.1   Constitutionality

The requirement that the attorney not give certain advice to his client appears to violate the First Amendment freedom of speech. For example, clients often ask whether they can purchase a new auto before filing or rent a new apartment. Section 526(a)(4) seems to mandate that the attorney not answer that question. Clearly the attorney cannot and should not advise the prospective debtor to run up his credit cards before filing but this section

---

[17] *Milavetz, Gallop & Milavetz v. U.S.A.*, 541 F.3d 785, (8th Cir. September 2008)(attorneys are debt relief agencies); *Hersh v. USA*, --- F.3d ----, 2008 WL 5255905 (5th Cir. December, 2008)

seems to go beyond that or at least chills the discussion between attorney and client.[18]

4. Disclosure Requirements of Debt Relief Agencies

A debt relief agency must provide to an assisted person a "clear and conspicuous written notice," within three days after first offering advice, informing the assisted person of a number of things. Section 527(a). In addition, the debt relief agency must provide the assisted person a "statement," "at the same time" as the first notice, "in a single document separate from other documents" a boilerplate statement "to the extent applicable, or one substantially similar," which is set forth at length in Section 527(b). Section 527(b). The debt relief agency is required to keep a copy of the notices for 2 years.

5. Additional Requirements for Debt Relief Agencies

A debt relief agency must have a written agreement with the assisted person "within five days" and prior to the bankruptcy filing in any event. Section 528

The debt relief agency must include the words "We are a debt relief agency. We help people file for bankruptcy relief under the Bankruptcy Code," or a "substantially similar statement" in any advertising directed to the general public. Some attorneys believe that this does not apply to advertising in a magazine directed to attorneys and not "the general public."

6. Consequences of Violating the Debt Relief Agency Rules

The consequence of violating the new debt relief agency rules is that the contract with the client is "void" and may not be enforced except by the assisted person. Section 527(C)(1).

In addition, the attorney is liable to the client for the fees charged, for actual damages, and for attorneys fees if the attorney, 1) intentionally or negligently failed to comply with these sections, 2) failed to file a document required which resulted in dismissal or conversion of the case, or, 3)

---

[18] Id. The *Milavetz* court ruled that this speech restriction is not unconstitutional. The Supreme Court has granted certiorari in *Milavetz*. Oral argument should take place in October, 2009.

disregarded the "material requirements" of the code, or the F.R.B.P. Section 527(C)(2).

PART TWO   THE DOOR TO CHAPTER 7: MEANS TESTING AND ABUSE

A Summary of Bankruptcy Law

5.   QUALIFYING FOR CHAPTER 7: BAD FAITH AND ABUSE

1.   Introduction

A chapter 7 bankruptcy case may be dismissed by the court for "cause," Section 707(a), or for "abuse," Section 707(b). Cause under Section 707(a) tends to be associated with "bad faith" and applies to any chapter 7 debtor. Abuse under Section 707(b) is limited to consumer cases and arises out of the concept that consumers who have the ability to pay a meaningful portion of their debts should not be allowed to simply file chapter 7 and receive a discharge without making any payments to their creditors.

1.1   Motion Required

Irrespective of the basis for the dismissal, a motion setting forth the basis for the requested dismissal must be filed by the party seeking dismissal with adequate notice to the debtor and creditors. The debtor, of course, is permitted to oppose the motion and explain why the case should not be dismissed. The trustee and creditors likewise have standing to object to the dismissal although that is rare unless there are assets to be liquidated and distributed to creditors.[19]

1.2   Voluntary Dismissal

Dismissal of a chapter 7 case at the request of the debtor requires a motion and notice to creditors setting forth the basis for the requested dismissal. Section 707(a) These motions are typically denied if the trustee or any other party in interest opposes the motion.

2.   Cause

The Bankruptcy Code sets forth three specific instances of "cause": failure to pay the fees, failure to file all the schedules, and "unreasonable

---

[19] *Wirum v. Warren (In re Warren)*, ---- F. 3d ----, 2009 WL 1694188 (9th Cir. June, 2009)(dismissal of case denied after trustee objected)

delay which is prejudicial to creditors." Section 707(a) Courts have determined over the years that cause also includes bad faith, although the Code does not expressly provide that as a basis for dismissal.[20]

2.1 Bad Faith

Cases have been dismissed forever for "bad faith" even though good faith was not required by the Bankruptcy Code until the 2005 amendments. Bad faith is not defined in the code. The cases however are clear that a bankruptcy case can be dismissed for lack of good faith ("a bad faith filing").

Bad faith is filing a bankruptcy petition for some purpose other than to obtain the legitimate benefits of the bankruptcy code. The legitimate purpose of bankruptcy is to obtain the discharge and the orderly distribution of the debtor's assets or the value of those assets. Bad faith filings include:

1) Multiple filings. A filing followed by a dismissal of the case followed by another filing. Sometimes a husband will file and his wife will file immediately after hubby's case is either dismissed or relief is granted to some creditor. Wife files to get more time to do whatever they are trying to do.

2) A transfer of property to an entity which then files a bankruptcy chapter, commonly called the "new debtor syndrome." For example, real property is transferred to a new or defunct corporation which then files bankruptcy. A more egregious example is where 10% of a piece of real property is transferred to each of 10 different individuals who then file bankruptcy one by one.

3) A chapter 11 filing with no intention to reorganize. Sometimes a person or entity will file a chapter 11 to "buy time." Time is usually needed to negotiate with some lender, or steal rent from an apartment building, or delay eviction, or stop seizure procedures pending a transfer of assets.

---

[20] *In re Padilla*, 222 F.3d 1184 (9th Cir. 2000)(the court must find cause, not just bad faith; credit card bust out by consumer not cause under 707(a) but may be abuse under 707(b))

4) Two party litigation cases. This arises when two persons or entities have been engaged in litigation in state court. One party will file bankruptcy to gain a perceived advantage. The filing usually takes place to avoid a state court order, or some particular state court judge; to avoid posting a bond; or, to simply relitigate an issue which has been lost. These cases usually have few or no creditors or debt problems other than the state court litigants.

A bad faith filing will result in dismissal of the case and likely a bar on refiling and possibly sanctions to the attorney and or debtor.[21] Sometimes a court will consider a less drastic measure such as giving the complaining creditor relief from the automatic stay to proceed against the debtor instead of dismissing the case entirely.

3.   "Abuse" - pre-2005 BAPCPA Amendments

Section 707(b) was added to the bankruptcy code in 1984. It was essentially one sentence which provided that a Chapter 7 case could be dismissed if "granting relief would be a substantial abuse" of the bankruptcy code. This meant generally that when the debtor had the ability, usually through earning power, to pay some significant portion of his or her debts, allowing the chapter 7 to proceed would amount to a substantial abuse and the case would be dismissed.[22] Most courts also applied a "totality of the circumstances" test using a myriad of factors to determine on a case-by-case basis whether the Chapter 7 filing amounted to a substantial abuse.[23] The motion to dismiss before BAPCPA could be brought only by the U.S. Trustee's Office. Section 707(b).

4.   "Abuse" - post-2005 Amendments

Responding to pressures from the credit card industry, BAPCPA replaced the single paragraph in Section 707(b) with several pages of rules designed to *quantify* whether or not the consumer debtor had the ability to

---

[21] *In re Rainbow Magazine, Inc.*, 136 B.R. 545 (9th Cir. BAP 1992)($261,000 in sanctions reversed)

[22] *In re Kelly*, 841 F.2d 908 (9th Cir. 1988)(ability to repay debts is basis for dismissal as an abuse)

[23] *In re Price*, 353 F.3d 1135 (9th Cir. 2005)(courts should look to totality of the circumstances when determining whether abuse exists)

repay a substantial portion of her debts. The stated purpose was to remove the uncertainties perceived in allowing courts to determine abuse on a case by case basis. This has come to be known as the "means test" and will be dealt with in some detail in the next chapters.

5. Abuse Test Applies only to Consumer Debtors

Section 707(b) applies by its terms only to individual "consumer debtors," that is, debtors whose debts are primarily consumer debts. The subsection cannot be used as a basis to dismiss the chapter 7 case of an individual debtors whose debts are primarily business debts. The business debtor's case may only be dismissed under Section 707(a).[24]

6. Bar on Refiling After Dismissal

Dismissal of a case does not generally prevent the debtor from immediately filing a new case. Section 349. The code does however provide that a person may not file a new bankruptcy petition for six months if the prior case was dismissed for willful failure to follow the rules or if a prior case was voluntarily dismissed after a creditor filed a Motion for Relief from Stay. Section 109(g)

6.1 Enforcement of Section 109(g) in the Central District

When a bankruptcy case is dismissed because the debtor failed to file all of the schedules or failed to appear at the First Meeting of Creditors, it is typically dismissed with a Section 109(g) bar on refiling for six months.

7. Dismissal with Prejudice

While rare, a court may dismiss a bankruptcy case "with prejudice."[25] What this means is not clear but the cases where dismissal with prejudice has occurred, the order typically provides that a subsequent filing will not result in a discharge of any debt that could have been discharged in the case being dismissed. The authority for dismissal with prejudice comes from Section 349 which states that "unless otherwise

---

[24] *In re Perlin,* 497 F.3d 364 (3rd Cir. August, 2007)(no cause to dismiss even though debtor had $400,000 in annual income)
[25] *In re Leavitt,* 171 F.3d 1219, 1223 (9th Cir.1999)

ordered" a dismissal does not bar refiling or a discharge of debts which were otherwise dischargeable at the time.

8. Limited Automatic Stay When Case is Refiled

When an individual debtor refiles a new case within one year of dismissal of a previous case, the automatic stays terminates "with respect to the debtor" 30 days after the second case is filed. Section 362(c)(3)(A) The debtor may request the court to extend the stay on a showing that the new case was filed "in good faith of the creditors stayed." Section 362(c)(3)(B)

When there has been two or more cases filed by the debtor and dismissed within the past year, the stay does "not go into effect." Section 362(c)(4)(a) Again, the debtor can move the court for a stay on a showing of good faith. Section 362(c)(4)(b)

The stay with respect to the estate apparently does not automatically terminate as the code states that it terminates "with respect to the debtor."

8.1 Good Faith

What is "presumptively not in good faith" is set forth in Section 362(c)(3)(C) and (c)(4)(D). For example when there has been more than one or two filings in the past year, or no "change of financial circumstances" or when the previous case was dismissed for failure to file all the forms.

6. OVERVIEW OF ABUSE IN CONSUMER CHAPTER 7 - SECTION 707(b)

1. Introduction

The test for dismissal in an individual chapter 7 consumer case is simple abuse. Section 707(b)(1) The court may dismiss a case for abuse. Abuse is determined by use of a "means test" in Section 707(b)(2) or by the "totality of the circumstances" in section 707(b)(3).

Congress has set forth in Section 707(b)(2) an elaborate "means test," a series of calculations under which a chapter 7 case is *presumed* to be an abuse or not. It has arisen out of the concept that those consumer who have the ability to pay a meaningful portion of their debts should not be able to simply file chapter 7 and receive a discharge without making any further payments to their creditors.

1.1 United States Trustee

The most active player in the filing of motions to dismiss for abuse is the US Trustee. Often the UST will request further information from the debtor such as bank statements, credit card statements, and the like before making the determination of whether or not to file a motion. The UST will likely appear at the meeting of creditors and question the debtor when it believes that there may be a basis to file a motion to dismiss for abuse.

2. Application to Persons Whose Debts are Primarily Consumer Debts

The means test and the concept of abuse under Section 707(b) applies only to individuals whose debts are "primarily consumer debts." Section 707(b)(1)

2.1 Consumer Debt Defined

Consumer debt is defined as a debt incurred primarily for the debtor's "personal, household or family purpose." Section 101(8). Case law has made it clear that a consumer debt is any debt not incurred with a profit motive.

2.2 Mortgages and Taxes

A home mortgage is a consumer debt[26] unless the funds were used in a business. Income taxes are not consumer debts.[27] Some courts have found that tort damages are not consumer debts.

3. "Above Median" Debtors

The means test applies only to individuals whose gross income is above the median income of his state for his or her particular household

---

[26] *In re Kelly*, 841 F.2d 908 (9th Cir. 1988)
[27] *In re Westberry*, 215 F.3d 589 (6th Cir. 2000)

size. Section 707(b)(7) In other words, it is *presumed* that filing the case is not an abuse under the means test if the debtor's income is under the median income for his household size in his state. The under-median case can still be dismissed as an abuse under the totality of the circumstances. Section 707(b)(3)

3.1 Income

The determination of whether a debtor is over or under the median in his state is based on the debtor (and his spouse's and sometimes other family members) "current monthly income." Section 707(b)(7) Current monthly income is the debtor's actual gross income for the past six calendar months. It includes "income from all sources" whether or not it is taxable. It includes any amounts "paid by any entity . . . on a regular basis to the debtor for household expenses." Section 101(10A) Social security income however is specifically excluded.

3.2 Household Size

Unfortunately there is no definition of household in the code. As I understand it, the UST will not object to the inclusion of any person in the household whom the debtor may take as a dependant on their personal tax returns. This is a very murky area however. Most attorneys believe that the debtor's live-in girlfriend and her children are members of the debtor's household even though they cannot be deducted as dependants on the debtor's tax return.

3.3 California Median Income

If the debtor is "in a household of one," the median family income in California is roughly $49,182 as of March 15, 2009. For a household of two, $65,097, three $70,684 and four $79,971. After four, add $6,900 for each additional individual in the household.[28]

---

[28] www.usdoj.gov/ust/eo/bapcpa/20090315/bci_data/median_income_table.htm

4. Means Test Raises a Presumption of Abuse and Therefore Dismissal

Failure to "pass" the means test results in a presumption that the case is an abusive filing and should be dismissed. The debtor may overcome the presumption with a showing that there are "special circumstances" which overcome the presumption that his case is an abuse of the bankruptcy process. Section 707(b)(2)(B)

5. Who May File a Section 707(b) Motion

Generally, any party in interest, the U.S. Trustee, or the court *sua sponte* may file a motion seeking dismissal under Section 707(b). If the debtor's income is under the median of his state, only the U.S. Trustee or the court may file the motion to dismiss and that motion may not be based on means testing. Section 707(b)(6)

6. Totality of the Circumstances

If abuse is not presumed under the means test (or is rebutted), the court may still find abuse and dismiss the case. Section 707(b)(3) In considering whether there is an abuse, the court "shall consider" whether or not the case was filed "in bad faith," or whether "the totality of the circumstances . . . of the debtor's financial circumstances demonstrates abuse."

In the 9th Circuit, courts are permitted to look to a number of "factors"[29] to determine whether or not there is abuse under the totality of the circumstances including:

(1) Whether the debtor has a likelihood of sufficient future income to fund a Chapter 11, 12, or 13 plan which would pay a substantial portion of the unsecured claims;

(2) Whether the debtor's petition was filed as a consequence of illness, disability, unemployment, or some other calamity;

---

[29] *In re Price*, 353 F.3d 1135 (9th Cir 2005). See criticism of *Price* in M. Jonathan Hayes, *Chapter 7 Bad Faith, Substantial Abuse and Dismissal with Prejudice; Totality of the Circumstances Needs to be Rethunk*, California Bankruptcy Journal, (Vol.24, No. 4, 2005)

(3) Whether the schedules suggest the debtor obtained cash advancements and consumer goods on credit exceeding his or her ability to repay them;

(4) Whether the debtor's proposed family budget is excessive or extravagant;

(5) Whether the debtor's statement of income and expenses is misrepresentative of the debtor's financial condition; and

(6) Whether the debtor has engaged in eve-of-bankruptcy purchases.[30]

The difficulty in the area of totality of the circumstances is the debtor who passes the means test under Section 707(b)(2) but whose "allowed" deductions under the means test are deemed by the court or the UST to be extravagant. For example, the debtor with a very large mortgage will often pass the means test even with very high income. This should not be the basis for dismissal under totality of the circumstances because it is specifically allowed under the means test.[31] These battles are not over as there is little consensus among the courts.

7. MEANS TESTING IN CHAPTER 7 –THE COMPUTATIONS

1. Introduction

There is a presumption of abuse in chapter 7 when the individual debtor (who is an "over-median income debtor" and whose debts are primarily consumer debts) fails to "pass" the means test set forth in Section 707(b)(2).

---

[30] Id.
[31] *In re Jensen,* 2:08-bk-15225ER (unpublished)(Bkrtcy, C.D. Cal. Robles J.); *In re Johnson,* --- B.R. ---, 2008 WL 5265740 (Bkrtcy, S.D.Cal. Dec. 2008, Bowie. J.)

2.   The Means Test

The basic computation begins with the individual debtor's "current monthly income," i.e., gross income received in the six calendar months before the bankruptcy filing. Section 101(10A) If this current monthly income exceeds *allowed* expenses (and other allowed deductions and payments) by more than $100 per month, abuse is presumed unless the excess per month multiplied by 60 will not pay at least 25% of the debtor's non priority unsecured claims. If the individual debtor's current monthly income exceeds expenses by more than $182.50 per month, abuse is presumed irrespective of the percentage of debts the monthly income will pay. Stated another way, if the net monthly income is more than $182.50 per month, abuse is presumed. If the net monthly income is less than $100 per month, the debtor "passes" the means test which therefore cannot be the basis for a motion to dismiss. If the net monthly income is between $100 and $182.50, abuse is presumed only if the total net monthly income for 60 months would pay more than 25% of the debtor's unsecured debts. Section 707(B)(2)

2.1 The Means Test Conceptually

It is helpful to think of the means test on a conceptual level before getting into the details. The computations typically do not result in any meaningful number. It quickly becomes obvious that although called "net monthly income," the result of the computations is typically an artificial number. If the end result of the means test computations is $200 per month, that does not necessarily mean in reality that the debtor can pay $200 per month to his creditors or into a chapter 13 plan. It simply means that there is a presumption of abuse and therefore the chapter 7 case will be dismissed unless the presumption is overcome.

3.   Current Monthly Income ("CMI")

The debtor's "current monthly income" is the average monthly income received from all sources in the six months prior to the bankruptcy filing. Section 101(10A) The receipt does not have to be taxable income to be included, for example, child support is included in CMI. Current monthly income includes all payments made by any person or entity "on a regular basis" for the debtor's household expenses. Current monthly income does not include "benefits paid under the Social Security Act."

3.1 No Consensus on CMI

This is also an area where there is significant dispute among attorneys and courts. If the debtor sells his truck during the six months, is the gross sales price included in CMI? Or the net proceeds? Or any portion of the receipt? If he sells stock, is the gross amount or the net profit included?

4.   Monthly Expenses

There are five categories of allowed expenses (or deductions from currently monthly income);

     a)   expenses according to certain charts,
     b)   certain "necessary expenses" in addition to the charts,
     c)   payments to secured creditors,
     d)   payments of priority claims,
     e)   expenses for "special circumstances."

5.   The Charts

The first level of allowed expenses is the amount specified in different charts published by the IRS.[32] They are:

- National Standards: food, clothing and other items.
- National Standards: health care.
- Local Standards: housing and utilities.
- Local Standards: housing and utilities; mortgage/rent expense.
- Local Standards: transportation; vehicle operation/public transportation expense.
- Local Standards: transportation ownership/lease expense.

6.   Amounts Allowed in Addition to the Charts

Certain amounts are allowed as deductions in addition to the charts.

---

[32] These charts can be found at www.usdoj.gov/ust.

Insurance: In addition to the charts, the debtor may deduct "reasonably necessary" medical insurance, disability insurance and health savings account expenses. Section 707(b)(2)(A)(ii)(I).

Safety Expenses: The debtor may also deduct "reasonably necessary" expenses "incurred to maintain the safety of the debtor from family violence (as defined therein)." Section 707(b)(2)(A)(ii)(I).

Additional food and clothing: The debtor may include an amount of up to 5% over the National Standards for food and clothing if "it is demonstrated that it is reasonable and necessary." Section 707(b)(2)(A)(ii)(I).

Care of disabled, ill or elderly: The debtor may include "the continuation of actual expenses" to care for "an elderly, chronically, ill, or disabled" member of the household or the debtor's family if that person is not able to pay to care for themselves. Section 707(b)(2)(A)(ii)(II).

Chapter 13 expenses: If the debtor is eligible for chapter 13, the debtor may deduct the projected trustee's monthly fee of up to ten percent of the projected plan payments. Section 707(b)(2)(A)(ii)(III).

Education: The debtor may deduct actual expenses up to a total of $1,650 per year per child "less than 18 years of age" for public or private education. The debtor must provide "a detailed explanation of why such expenses are reasonable and necessary and why such expenses are not already accounted for" in the IRS charts. Section 707(b)(2)(A)(ii)(IV).

Excess housing expenses: The debtor may deduct actual expenses for "home energy costs" in excess of the Local Standards (IRS chart). The debtor must "provide documentation of such actual expenses and demonstrates that such expenses are reasonable and necessary." Section 707(b)(2)(A)(ii)(V).

There are several other categories of expenses allowed to be deducted on the means test such as charitable contributions, expenses for "protection against family violence," and others.

7.   Payments to Secured Creditors

The debtor may deduct payments made "on account of secured debts." The amount to be deducted is the total amount "scheduled as contractually due" to secured creditors for the next 60 months divided by 60. The debtor may also deduct "additional payments to secured creditors" for the debtor's "primary residence, motor vehicle, or other property necessary for the support of the debtor . . . divided by 60." Section 707(b)(2)(A)(iii).

7.1 Example

Assume the debtor is paying $600 per month on an auto loan on which he has 20 more payments before it is paid off. The deduction on the means test would be $200, i.e., $600 times 20 equals $12,000 divided by 60 or $200.

7.2 Secured Debts the Debtor Does Not Intend to Pay

The debtor has a choice with respect to postpetition payment of secured debts. He may continue to make the payments and retain the property or he may return the property and the debt is discharged. Some courts have held that the debtor may not deduct on the means test payments for secured debts he does not intend to make, i.e., for property he intends to return.[33] Other courts have ruled that whether the payments may be deducted for purposes of the means test or not, the decision to return the property and avoid the payment is an important factor when looking at the totality of the circumstances under Section 707(b)(3).[34]

7.3 Example

Suppose the debtor has a $3,000 monthly mortgage payment. Suppose also that after deducting the mortgage payment on the means test, the debtor's net disposable income is minus $2,000. The debtor passes the means test but some courts rule that the payment cannot be deducted and therefore the debtor does not pass the means test. Other courts rule that the debtor passes the means test but under the totality of the circumstances, the debtor

---

[33] *In re Wilkins*, 370 B.R. 815 (Bkrtcy C.D.Cal. 2007)(payments may be deducted from the means test even if the debtor intends to return the property)
[34] *In re Baeza*, 398 B.R. 392 (Bkrtcy, E.D.Cal Dec. 2008, Lee. J.)(debtor's intent to surrender collateral leaving substantial net disposable income is grounds to dismiss under Section 707(b)(3))

can pay $1,000 per month because she is giving up the home and a chapter 7 is therefore an abuse and must be dismissed.

7.4   No Deduction for Repayment of Secured Debts Owing to the Debtor's IRA or 401(k) Plans

Repayment of loans made against retirement plans may not be deducted on the means test.[35]

7.5   No "Double-Dipping"

The IRS "Local Standards: housing and utilities; mortgage/rent expense" chart includes, presumably, some standard amount for mortgages.   The means test seemingly permits deduction of the chart amount and also deduction of the mortgage. The means test form requires that the chart amount be reduced by the mortgage payment. The same applies to the vehicle ownership deduction.

7.5.1 Vehicle Ownership Deduction

Some courts will not allow the debtor to take the amount in the "Vehicle Ownership" chart if the debtor is not making payments to an auto lender under the assumption that the amount in the chart is supposed to cover the purchase price payments and cannot be deducted if the vehicle is owned outright by the debtor. The form again requires that the ownership deduction must be reduced by the monthly payment so that there is no "double-dipping."

8.   Priority Expenses

The debtor may deduct, in addition to the other deductions, payment of all priority claims including child support and alimony.   The debtor has to total the priority payments owed for the next 60 months and divide by 60. Presumably this includes payroll and income taxes since those taxes do not appear in any of the other categories.   Section 707(b)(2)(A)(iv)

---

[35] *In re Egebjerg*, ---- F. 3d ----, 2009 WL 1492138 (9th Cir. May, 2009)

8.1 Income Taxes

The means test does not include specifically a deduction for current income taxes paid on current monthly income. The means test form permits that deduction however under "other necessary deductions."

9. "Special Circumstances"

The debtor may overcome the presumption of abuse based on means testing by showing "special circumstances, such as a serious medical condition or an order to active duty in the Armed Forces." To show special circumstances, the debtor must "justify additional expenses or adjustments of current monthly income for which there is no reasonable alternative." The debtor must set forth documentation and give a detailed explanation of these special circumstances. Special circumstances do not apply unless the additional expenses drop the debtor's net monthly income below $167 per month, or between $100 and $182.50 if the net would not pay at least 25% of non priority debts, or under $100 irrespective of the amount of debts that amount would pay. Section 707(b)(2)(B)

10. No Deductions for Retirement Accounts

There is no deduction allowed for payments made to retirement accounts such as 401(k) plans or I.R.A.s.

8. MEANS TESTING IN CHAPTER 7 – THE PROCEDURE

1. The Means Test Form

The means test form, form B22, is several pages long and must be filed by the debtor with his schedules.[36] The top of the first page of the B22 has two boxes, one of which must be checked. The boxes state that this case is a "presumed abuse case," i.e., the debtor failed the means test, or that "no presumption arises," i.e., the debtor passes the means test.

---

[36] I'm not sure I could complete this form properly myself without a bankruptcy forms computer program.

1.1 Non-Consumer and Under-Median Cases

It is not clear whether the B22 form is required when the debtor's debts are primarily business debts or whose income is below the median of his state. Practitioners should however include the form and indicate on the first page that it does not apply and the reason why.

2. Duty of US Trustee to Review Every Chapter 7

The US Trustee is required by the code to "review all of the materials filed by the debtor," and within 10 days after "the date of the first meeting of creditors," file with the court a "statement" saying whether or not the debtor's chapter 7 is presumed to be an abuse under the means testing standards. Section 704(b)(1) This apparently applies even if the debtor's income is below the median income of his state. The court then is required to "provide a copy of the statement to all creditors" within five days after receipt.

3. Duty of the US Trustee to File Section 707(b) Motions

If the U.S. Trustee has determined in its statement that abuse is presumed, it must, within 30 days after filing the statement, file a Motion to Dismiss the case under Section 707(b), or, file a second "statement setting forth the reasons" it "does not consider such a motion to be appropriate." No motion or second statement is required if the debtor's income is below the median income of his state. Section 704(b)(2)

4. Rights of Other "Parties in Interest" to File Section 707(b) Motions

Any "party in interest" may file a Motion to Dismiss a chapter 7 at any time during the case. Section 707(b)(1) Only the UST may file a motion to dismiss if the debtor is a "below median debtor." Section 707(b)(6)

5. Motion Required

If the U.S. Trustee determines that there is abuse, it will file a Motion to Dismiss the case. Typically a hearing will take place about 30 days later. The motion begins a "contested proceeding" in which both parties, i.e., the debtor and the U.S. Trustee may conduct discovery, take depositions, demand documents etc.

5.1 Sanctions Against Counsel

Sanctions may be assessed "in accordance with the procedures described in F.R.B.P. 9011" against the attorney for the debtor if the case is dismissed and the requirements of F.R.B.P. 9011 are met.

6.   Conversion to Chapter 13

Typically when the court determines that an abuse exists, the court will advise the debtor that he has the right to convert the case to chapter 13 and if the case is so converted, it will not be dismissed. Section 706

A Summary of Bankruptcy Law

PART THREE   CHAPTER 7

9. BASIC CHAPTER 7 PROCEDURE

1. Commencement of the Case

A chapter 7 is commenced by the filing of a petition. Section 301 and 302 There is a filing fee of $299 unless the fee is waived. Along with the petition, there are a number of schedules which list the debtor's property, her debts, and claimed exemptions. These "schedules" include a statement of monthly income and expenses and a series of questions known as the "Statement of Financial Affairs." Section 521(a)(1)

2. After the Petition is Filed

A trustee is assigned to the case by the court clerk when the case is filed. Section 701 and 702. The trustee's job is to seize all property of the debtor that has equity which is not exempt, sell it and distribute the money to the creditors. Section 704. The trustee typically also investigates prepetition transfers of property by the debtor to determine if the transfer can be unwound and the property returned by the transferee. The vast majority of all chapter 7 cases are "no asset" cases, meaning the debtor owns no non-exempt property with equity.

2.1 Notice to Creditors

When the case is filed, the court clerk sends a notice of the filing of the case to all of the creditors listed by the debtor in the schedules. The notice provides the name of the trustee, the date and location of the first meeting of creditors and other information including the last date by which creditors may object to the discharge.

3. The First Meeting of Creditors

The first meeting of creditors usually takes place three to five weeks after the case is filed.[37] Section 341(a) It is conducted by the trustee assigned to the case in a meeting room at the U.S. Trustee's Office. The

---

[37] Rule 2003

trustee typically asks a few questions regarding the schedules that have been filed and the meeting is concluded. Sometimes the trustee will ask for documents such as financial statements for a business, bank statements, or information regarding sales of property in the past and will continue the meeting to allow the returns to be provided. Creditors typically do not appear at the meeting and when they, do, are allowed to ask only a few questions about the debtor's assets. The U.S. Trustee will, on occasion, attend the meeting and question the debtor typically seeking information to determine whether or not a motion should be filed seeking dismissal for abuse.

4.   Statement of Intentions: Secured Creditors

The debtor must file, within 30 days of filing the petition, a statement of intention with respect to personal property which is subject to a purchase money security interest, i.e., when the property is some creditor's "collateral." Section 521(a)(2)(A) The debtor must perform that intention within 30 days after the first meeting of creditors. Section 521(a)(2)(B) This means that the debtor must enter into a reaffirmation agreement with the secured creditor under Section 524(c), or redeem the personal property pursuant to Section 722. If the debtor does neither, he must return the collateral to the secured creditor within 45 days of the first meeting of creditors. If the debtor does not reaffirm or redeem, the automatic stay is terminated automatically with respect to the property and the property is no longer property of the estate under Section 541(a). Section 362(h)

5.   Providing Tax Returns

The debtor "shall provide" to the trustee, at least 7 days before the meeting of creditors, a copy of the debtor's most recent year's tax return or a "transcript of such return." At the same time the debtor must provide a copy of the return or transcript to any creditor who requests it. Section 521(e)(2) It is not clear what a "transcript" is although the IRS provides upon request of the taxpayer a form it calls a transcript.

5.1   Consequences of Failure to Provide Tax Return

If the debtor fails to provide the return or transcript, the court "shall dismiss the case" unless the debtor demonstrates that the failure was beyond his control. Section 521(2)(B) & (C)

5.2 Tax Returns Filed While the Bankruptcy is Pending

"At the request of the court, the US Trustee or any party in interest," the debtor "shall file with the court" any tax returns filed while the case is pending, and any amendments filed while the case is pending. Section 521(f)

5.3 Dismissal for Failure to File Tax Returns While Bankruptcy Case is Pending

If the debtor fails to file returns or obtain an extension for tax returns which come due during the case, the court may dismiss or convert the case "on request of the taxing authority." If the return is not filed within 90 days after the taxing authority "requests" the return, the court shall dismiss or convert the case. Section 521(j)

6. Automatic Dismissal for Failure to File All Required Forms

If the debtor fails to file all the forms required under Section 521(a)(1), the case is automatically dismissed on the 46th day after the petition date. Section 521(i) The debtor may seek an additional 45 days from the court if the court finds "justification for extending" the period. Also, at the request of the trustee, the court may "decline to dismiss the case."

7. Completion of the Personal Financial Management Program

In order to receive his discharge, the debtor must complete a personal financial management course "described in Section 111." Section 727(a)(11) A certificate must be filed by the debtor attesting to completion of this program. If the debtor does not file the attestation, he is in danger of having his case closed without entry of the discharge.

8. Giving Creditors an Opportunity to Object to the Discharge

Creditors may file a complaint asking the court to deny the discharge, Section 727, or to declare that a particular debt is non-dischargeable. Section 523. The last day to file these complaints is 60 days after the first date set for the first meeting of creditors.[38] This date can be extended only by the judge after a hearing. The trustee and the U.S. Trustee are also authorized to file complaints to deny the discharge. Section 727(c)(1) If no complaints regarding the discharge are filed, the discharge is "entered," effective as of the date of the petition. Section 727(b) Entry or lack of entry of the discharge does not affect the activities of the trustee.

9.   Closing the Case

Once the trustee determines that there are no assets to sell, the trustee will file a form with the court called a No Asset Report. The "report," a pre-printed one page form, is not sent to creditors. Once the time to object to the discharge has elapsed, and the trustee has filed the No Asset Report, the case is closed by the court clerk.

10.   Procedure When There are Assets

When there are assets to administer in a chapter 7 case, the trustee will usually retain an attorney to assist him. The trustee will ask the court clerk to give notice to creditors that they must file Proofs of Claim on or before a certain date. The trustee will file a motion asking the court to approve the sale of the asset. Section 363(b). The sale will be subject to overbids and the debtor may bid at the hearing. The sale may be free and clear of liens under some circumstances. Section 363(f) Often in these cases, the debtor is the purchaser and there are no overbidders. The trustee will then file an accounting, advise the court of the funds available to distribute and the case will be closed after that.

10.1 When the Debtor Owns an Operating Business

The bankruptcy code permits the trustee to operate a business only if the court approves the operation and then only for a limited period. Section 721 Trustees rarely operate the business for long. It is common for the trustee to close an operating business immediately.

---

[38] Rule 4004(a)

11.   Entry of Discharge and Closing of the Case

The entry of the debtor's discharge and the closing of the bankruptcy case have nothing to do with each other. The discharge is entered once the time to object to the discharge has run. If someone has objected to the discharge, the discharge is not entered until the objection is resolved.

The bankruptcy case, on the other hand, remains open and active until the trustee either files a "no asset report" advising the court there is nothing further to do in the case or until the trustee files a final accounting. The "no asset report" is typically filed within a week to several months after the first meeting of creditors, as soon as the trustee determines that there are no assets of the debtor which have equity and are not exempt. The final accounting is filed when the trustee has found and sold assets. The final accounting may be a year or two or more after the case begins.

12.   Conversion of the Chapter 7 Case to Another Chapter During the Case

The debtor is generally permitted to "convert" his case from chapter to 7 to chapter 13 or chapter 11.[39] Section 706   Creditors must be given notice and an opportunity to object to the conversion.

10.   PROPERTY OF THE ESTATE

1.   General

Immediately upon filing a petition under any chapter, an estate is created. Section 541(a). The estate consists of all of the legal and equitable interests of the debtor in property wherever located. This definition has been interpreted very broadly. Any rights which the debtor may have in property whether or not contingent, subject to restrictions, subject to the rights of co owners, difficult to value, or where the rights to enjoy are delayed, are all assets of the estate.

---

[39] Rule 1017(f)

1.1 The Great Wall of China

Only property or rights to property owned by the debtor at the moment of filing is included in the property of the chapter 7 estate. Property acquired after the filing is not property of the estate with the three exceptions set forth below.

1.2 Tangible Property

The debtor's bank accounts, clothes, furniture, automobile, residence, ownership in any business, pets, and other tangible property are all property of the estate. Much of this property is exempt as is set forth in the next chapter.

1.2.1 Leased Property

Property leased by the debtor, perhaps a vehicle or other equipment, is nevertheless property of the estate. It is more proper to say that the debtor's rights to possession and use of the property is property of the estate. These assets are generally known as executory contracts. If the trustee were to sell the debtor's rights, the buyer would have to take over the payments owing under the lease. For that reason, the lease has no value to the trustee unless the total payments to be made to the lessor is less that the value of the use of the property itself. This principle is the same if the debtor is leasing an apartment or space in a building. The lease payments to be made to the lessor would have to be less that the fair value of the space at the time for there to be any value to the estate.

1.2.2 Example.

Suppose the debtor rents office space under a very old lease for $1,000 per month. If the value of the space is $2,000 per month, someone would be willing to pay the trustee for the right to take over the lease.

1.2.3 Operating Businesses

Chapter 7 trustees rarely operate businesses, and therefore when the debtor owns a business as a sole proprietor, the trustee will typically close the business, and will certainly require proof of insurance to keep it open even for a short time.

1.3 Intangible Property

1.3.1 Litigation

If at the moment of the filing of the petition, the debtor has the right to sue someone, for example, his ex-boss, ex-wife, his attorney, or anyone else, that right belongs to the estate. It does not matter that no suit has been actually filed, the right to collect from the offender belongs to the estate. Often the trustee will abandon the right because he does not believe that the litigation is likely to generate funds for the estate, at least without significant effort or expense. The trustee may however retain counsel including the attorney who was handling the case for the debtor before filing. The proceeds of the litigation may be exempt and if so will likely be abandoned by the trustee.

1.3.2 Tax Rights

The right to a tax refund is property of the estate. The right to carryback a net operating loss ("NOL") is property of the estate.[40]

1.3.3 Property "Rooted in the Pre-bankruptcy Past"

Sometimes the debtor's right to receive a payment for his work depends on his pre-bankruptcy efforts as well as post-bankruptcy efforts. An example is commission earned by a real estate salesperson. If an escrow has been opened for a sale but does not close until after the bankruptcy filing, a portion of the later-earned commission belongs to the estate. The portion which is "rooted in the pre-bankruptcy past" belongs to the estate. How much that is, is a factual question. Another example is an attorney who takes a case on a contingency before he files

---

[40] *Segal v. Rochelle*, 382 U.S. 375 (1966)

his own bankruptcy. If he becomes entitled to a fee after the bankruptcy, a portion of the fee belongs to the bankruptcy estate.

2.   Property that is not Property of the Estate

Wages earned after the filing of a bankruptcy petition are not property of the estate in a chapter 7. Section 541(a)(6). Postpetition wages are property of the estate in a chapter 13 and chapter 11.

2.1 Property in a Spendthrift Trust

The debtor's rights in property held by a trust which includes a "spendthrift clause" are not property of the estate. Section 541(c)(2) This includes all ERISA qualified pension funds[41] since the trust documents always have spendthrift clauses. If the debtor however has any present right, at the moment of filing the case, to receive a payment or other property from the trust, the bankruptcy trustee may "stand at the door" and collect the proceeds coming out of the trust.

2.2 Corporate Property

When the debtor "owns" a corporation which itself owns a business or other property, only the debtor's stock is property of the estate. The assets of the corporation are not property of the estate. The trustee however, at the moment the individual's case is filed, becomes the shareholder and may choose to elect a new board of directors, fire the debtor, and dissolve the corporation. This is rare however unless the corporation owns a business or assets that have value and can be sold for more than the corporate debts. The trustee could, as the sole shareholder, cause the corporation to sell its assets or its business. The proceeds would be subject to the claims of the corporate creditors first however.

2.3 Piercing the Corporate Veil

The trustee will sometimes seek to "pierce the corporate veil" and bring the corporate assets into the individual shareholder's estate along with all the corporate debts. If the

---

[41] *Patterson v. Schumate*, 504 U.S. 753 (1992)

debtor is found to be the *alter ego* of the corporation, the property of the corporation would become property of the estate.

3.   Property Acquired Postpetition Which Becomes Property of the Estate

The following property becomes property of the estate even though it is acquired after filing a petition in bankruptcy: Section 541(a)(5).

1)   Inheritance which the debtor receives or becomes entitled to receive within six months after the petition is filed.

2)   Life insurance proceeds which the debtor receives or becomes entitled to receive within six months after the petition is filed.

3)   Property from a marital settlement agreement which the debtor receives or becomes entitled to receive within six months after the petition is filed.

4.   Determination of What is Property

The Bankruptcy Code does not define property. Property rights are determined according to state and other non-bankruptcy law.[42] Ownership issues arise often as the trustee may only sell property owned by the debtor. What is owned by the debtor or what rights she may have to property is determined typically by looking to state law or other non-bankruptcy law.

5.   Community Property

All community property is included in the property of the estate, even when only one spouse files a petition. Section 541(a)(2).

6.   Co-Owners of Property

Except when the property is community property, only the debtor's interest in the property is property of the estate. For example, when a debtor owns 20% of a building, or of a partnership which in turn owns the building, only the 20% interest is property of the estate.

---

[42] *Butner v. U.S.*, 440 U.S. 48 (1979)

6.1 Rights of Trustee to Sell Co-Owner's Interest

The trustee can ask the court for permission to sell the debtor's interest and the interests of the co-owners if a partition of the property is impracticable and if the sale of the debtor's interest would bring significantly less to the estate than a sale of the entire property. Section 363(h).

7. Property in the Possession of Another

Property in the possession of another including a state court appointed receiver or a creditor who has seized but not yet sold the property, must be turned over to the trustee immediately. Section 542 and 543.

8. Contractual Restrictions

If the property owned by the debtor is subject to restrictions upon transfer, the trustee is generally bound by these restrictions although the trustee may ask that the restriction be ignored if it unreasonably restricts the right of the trustee to sell the property.[43]

8.1 Example

Partnership agreements often provide that the partnership interest must be offered to the other partners before it can be sold to an outsider. That provision is binding on the trustee unless it unreasonably limits the ability of the trustee to sell the asset.

8.2 Unenforceable Restrictions

If a restriction matures only upon the filing of a bankruptcy case, the restriction will be ignored. Section 541(c)(1)(B)

9. Abandonment of Property of the Estate

The trustee may abandon property during the case if the property is "burdensome to the estate or of inconsequential value and benefit to the estate." Section 554. To do so, the trustee must give notice of his intent to

---

[43] *Chicago Board of Trade v. Johnson*, 264 U.S. 1 (1924)

do so and permit creditors to object if they wish.[44] This is rare. Typically, the property is not abandoned until the case is closed. On occasion, however the trustee will cooperate with abandonment.

9.1 Example

Assume the debtor is trying to sell her home. If there were no equity beyond the homestead exemption, the trustee would have no interest in the sale but technically it is property of the estate and may not be sold by the debtor until the estate is closed or the property is abandoned by the trustee.

10.   Appreciation of the Value of Property of the Estate During the Pendancy of the Case

Appreciation in the value of property of the estate during the administration of the estate belongs to the estate.[45] Section 541(a)(6) For example, if the debtor's residence has no equity above the homestead exemption when the case is filed but increases in value after the case is filed, the increase in value belongs to the estate and the trustee may sell the home notwithstanding the fact that the residence was claimed fully exempt on the petition date.[46]

10.1 Forcing the Trustee to Abandon the Property

The debtor should file a motion several months into the case asking the court to order the trustee to abandon a particular asset back to the debtor when the asset is increasing in value. The basis is that there is no value for the estate at the time of the motion. Section 554(b) The court typically will not order the trustee to abandon the property over the trustee's objection unless the trustee has had significant time to market and sell the property and has been unable to do so.

---

[44] Rule 6007, *Catalano v. CIR*, 279 F.3d 682 (9th Cir. 2002)(procedures under Section 554 must be followed before property is legally abandoned)
[45] *In re Vu*, 245 B.R. 644 (9th Cir. BAP 2000)
[46] *In re Chappell*, 373 B.R. 73 (9th Cir. BAP July, 2007)

10.2 Sales Years Later

There have been cases where the estate is not closed for one reason or the other for three or four years or more. If, during that time, the debtor's home has risen significantly in value, it is still property of the estate and may be sold by the trustee. Debtor's counsel must be vigilant and ask the court to order the trustee to abandon the residence after six months or so if the case is not closed by then.

11. Property in the Estate When the Case is Closed

Property which is not sold by the trustee is abandoned back to the debtor when the case is closed. Section 541(c)   Property is only abandoned during the case when there is a court order providing for the abandonment.

12. Property Not Disclosed to the Trustee

Property which is not disclosed to the trustee is not administered and is therefore not abandoned when the case is closed. Section 544(d) When the debtor fails to disclose the existence of an asset, the trustee is entitled to reopen the bankruptcy case to administer the asset.[47]

11.   EXEMPTIONS

1.   General

Federal and state law both provide that certain property of the debtor may not be seized by creditors or a chapter 7 trustee. This is called exempt property. Exempt property is property of the estate at the outset of the case.

1.1 No Priority Over Liens

Exemptions do not have priority over liens.   The exemption applies only to the equity in the property. Suppose an

---

[47] *First National Bank of Jacksboro v. Lasater*, 196 U.S. 115 (1905); *In re Pace*, 67 F.3d 187 (9th Cir. 1995)(unscheduled assets are neither abandoned or administered under Section 554)

auto is exempt up to $2,400. If the auto is worth $10,000 and there is a lien on the auto of $9,000, only the $1,000 of equity is exempt.

2.   Exemptions

The bankruptcy code provides that a debtor may choose to exempt property under either the exemptions provided in the bankruptcy code, Section 522(d), or the exemptions provided by the debtor's particular state.[48] Section 522(b)(1)   The code also permits individual states to "opt out" of the federal exemptions and require use of exemptions provided under that state's law. Section 522(b)(2). Most of the states have so opted out including California.[49]

In California, a debtor may choose between two lists both identified in the California Code of Civil Procedure ("C.C.P."). The first list is called the "federal" list because it generally follows Section 522(d) although with numerous differences. C.C.P. 703.140(b)   The second list is called the "state" list. C.C.P. 704 et seq. It is significantly longer and more expansive than the federal list. The debtor must choose between the two lists.[50] He cannot pick and choose between the two lists.

2.1 The "Federal List"

A general summary of the Federal List (arising out of California Law), C.C.P. Section 703.140(b)[51]

a) $20,725 on the debtor's principle residence. This is the federal homestead exemption. This exemption can, however, be used to exempt anything if the debtor does not have a home and thus does not need the homestead exemption. For this reason, this exemption is called the "wild-card" exemption;

b) $3,300 for one automobile;

---

[48] Rule 4003(a)

[49] Cal. C.C.P. 703.130

[50] Cal. C.C.P. 703.140(b) states: The debtor may use the exemptions "herein in lieu of all other exemptions provided by this chapter."

[51] The exemption amounts are increased every three years. C.C.P. 703.150. The next increase will take place on April 1, 2010.

c) $525 per item of household furniture, clothing, books, animals, musical instruments etc.;

d) $1,350 of jewelry;

e) $2,075 of tools of the trade;

f) Payments from pension plans to the extent needed by the debtor for his support;

g) Payments up to $20,725 for certain types of personal injury actions;

h) Numerous other items.

2.2 The State List

In California, the significant exemptions are as follows: C.C.P. Sections 704 et seq.

a) Homestead exemption on the debtor's principle residence of $50,000 for a single person; $75,000 for a married couple and other family units; and $150,000 for certain senior citizens. C.C.P. 704.730 This is not a wild card and thus may not be applied to other items if the debtor has no home to protect.

b) $2,550 for one automobile; C.C.P. 704.010

c) All household furnishings, wearing apparel and other personal effects if ordinarily and reasonably necessary to the debtor and his family.

d) $6,750 of tools of the trade (plus $6,750 for the spouse if the spouse has different tools of the trade); C.C.P. 704.060

e) $6,750 of jewelry; C.C.P. 704.040

f) $10,775 of cash surrender value in life insurance contracts; C.C.P. 704.100

g) Unemployment, disability or health insurance benefits, and workers' compensation claims or payments;

h) pension plan designed and used primarily for retirement purposes;[52] C.C.P. 704.115

i) many other items.

2.2.1 State Exemptions Outside of Bankruptcy

The exemptions under the state list, i.e., C.C.P. 704 et seq, apply whether the debtor has filed bankruptcy or not.

2.3 Limitation on the Homestead Exemption

When a debtor has owned his residence for less than three and one half years (1210 days), the homestead exemption is limited to $125,000. Section 522(p)

2.4 Individual Retirement Accounts

In addition to the above lists, Individual Retirement Accounts ("IRA") are exempt up to $1,095,000 million. Section 522(n)

2.5 Pension Funds in General

Pension funds which are "ERISA Qualified" are not property of the estate because property of the estate does not include any property in a "spendthrift trust."[53] Section 541(c)(2)

3. Claiming the Exemptions

These exemptions are claimed by the debtor on Schedule C in the schedules filed with his bankruptcy petition. Section 522(l) The courts are generally casual about allowing the debtor to amend this schedule after the case has been filed.

---

[52] *In re Rucker,* --- F.3d ---, 2009 WL -------- (9th Cir. 2009)(debtor's purpose was to hide assets, not to have assets for retirement); *In re Jacoway,* 255 B.R. 234 (9th Cir. BAP 2000)(non-exhaustive list of factors for determining the purpose for the creation of the pension plan)

[53] *Paterson v. Schumate,* 504 U.S. 753 (1992)(ERISA qualified pensions not property of the estate because of the spendthrift clause in the instrument creating the pension)

3.1 Is the Asset Exempt or a Certain Value in the Asset?

In the 9th Circuit, only the amount of the exemption claimed in an asset is exempt. The asset itself is not exempt.[54] For example, if the debtor claims his auto exempt in the amount of $2,000, only that $2,000 is exempt. The trustee can still sell the auto if he can find a buyer. The debtor would receive the $2,000 claimed exemption from the sale. The 3rd Circuit has ruled that the asset itself is exempt when the debtor claims the full amount of equity exempt unless the trustee timely objects to the claimed exemption.[55]

4.   Objecting to the Exemptions

The trustee or any creditor has 30 days after the conclusion of the first meeting of creditors to object to the exemptions.[56]   The Supreme Court has ruled that the exemption claimed by the debtor cannot be attacked after this deadline runs no matter how clear it is that the claimed exemption is wrong or does not otherwise apply.[57]

4.1 Effect of Continuance of Meeting of Creditors

The 30 day deadline does not begin until the meeting of creditors is concluded. It is common for trustees to "continue" the meeting to review documents or further investigate something. It is not uncommon for the meeting to be continued many times for the sole purpose of delaying the time when the trustee must object to the exemption.

5.   Exemptions of Married Couples

A husband and wife are entitled to each exemption only once unless the specific exemption provides that it applies to both husband and wife. Section 522(b)(1)

---

[54] *In re Chappell*, 373 B.R. 73 (9th Cir. BAP July, 2007); *In re Hymen*, 967 F.2d 1316 (9th Cir. 1992).

[55] *Schwab v. Reilly (In re Reilly)*, 534 F.3d 173 (3rd Cir, July 2008). The Supreme Court has granted cert in *Reilly* to resolve the issue which now divides the circuits. Oral arguments are expected to take place in November, 2009.

[56] Rule 4003(b)

[57] *Taylor v. Freeland & Kronz*, 503 U.S. 638 (1992)

5.1 Example

For example, tools of the trade are exempt up to $6,750 or $13,500 if both husband and wife have tools of the trade. But the couple may exempt only one vehicle. If only the husband files, he may exempt the vehicle. If the wife files later, she may not exempt another vehicle.

6. Changing States to Obtain Better Exemptions

State exemptions vary wildly between states. For example, five states provide an *unlimited* homestead exemption and approximately 25 states provide a homestead exemption of $25,000 or less. This has led to people moving from one state to another for the sole purpose of obtaining the more favorable exemption scheme of the new state.

The 2005 amendments addressed this perceived abuse by providing that the debtor must claim the exemption of the state in which he lived in the two years prior to filing the petition. If the debtor did not live in one state for two consecutive years prior to filing, he must use the exemptions of the state in which he lived the 180 days (or the majority of the 180 days) *before* the two years before the bankruptcy filing. Section 522(b)(3)(A)

6.1 Example

Assume the debtor moved from Montana to California one year before filing his bankruptcy petition. He would not be able to use California's exemptions because he did not live there for two years before filing. He would have to use Montana exemptions provided he lived in Montana for 180 days prior to two years before the bankruptcy filing. If he did not live in Montana for 180 days before two years before the filing, he would use the state where he lived for the longer portion of the 180 days than any other state.

7. Conversion of Non-exempt Assets into Exempt Assets on the Eve of Filing

The existence of pre-bankruptcy planning is acknowledged in the legislative history to the 1978 Bankruptcy Act: "As under current law, the debtor will be permitted to convert nonexempt property into exempt property before filing a bankruptcy petition." The practice is not fraudulent as to creditors and permits the debtor to use of the exemptions to which he is entitled under law. In fact, it is probably the responsibility of counsel for the debtor to advise the prospective debtor of the use of conversion of non-exempt assets into exempt assets.

Unfortunately, this conversion process sometimes results in denial of the discharge for fraudulently transferring assets within one year of filing. Section 727(a)(2)

7.1 Example

The debtor may take $2,000 of non-exempt cash and open an exempt IRA account immediately prior to filing. Cash is not exempt unless it is exempted under the wild card exemption in the Federal List. The debtor may sell a non-exempt vehicle and buy exempt household furniture on the eve of filing.

8. Avoidance of Liens Which Impair Exemptions

Security interests and liens survive bankruptcy with almost no exceptions. One of the few exceptions is certain liens which impair an exemption. The following liens may be avoided to the extent that the lien impairs an exemption:

a) judgment liens;

b) Non-purchase money, non-possessory security interests in household goods, clothing, tools, health aids, and the like. The code lists what property qualifies as "household goods," for example, "1 television," "1 VCR." Section 522(f)(4)(A)

8.1 Example – Real Property

Suppose the debtor's home is worth $200,000 on the date of filing and there is a mortgage of $150,000. The $50,000 of equity is exempt under the California homestead exemption. If American Express has obtained a judgment against the debtor for $20,000 for example and has recorded an abstract, it has a lien on the home which impairs the $50,000 exemption and the lien will be avoided.

8.2 Example - Personal Property

Suppose the debtor's furniture is worth $1,000 on the date of filing. If Sears has a lien on the furniture because the furniture was purchased with a Sears credit card, the lien is a purchase money lien and may not be avoided. If however, the debtor went to a finance company and obtained a loan and put up the furniture as collateral, that lien will be avoided since it is a non-purchase money, non-possessory lien on property which is listed in the code and would otherwise be exempt.

8.3 Computing the Extent to Which the Lien Impairs the Exemption

The lien impairs the exemption, "to the extent that the lien, all other liens on the property and the exemption if there were no liens exceeds the value of the property." Section 522(f)(2)

8.3.1 Tax Liens and Liens Securing Alimony Debt

Tax liens are not "judgment liens" and cannot therefore be avoided under Section 522(f). Liens which secure alimony may not be avoided under Section 522(f). Section 522(f)(A)

8.4 Motion Required

A motion must be filed by the debtor in order to avoid the lien under this section. It does not happen automatically.

9. Exempting Property Recovered by the Trustee

Property which the trustee recovers typically through preference actions or avoiding fraudulent conveyance actions may not be exempted once the property is returned to the estate. Section 522(g) This rule does not apply when the transfer by the debtor was not voluntary, i.e., the property was seized by the creditor prepetition.

9.1 Example

Suppose the debtor transfers his home to his mother for no consideration. The home is not property of the estate when the case is filed because the debtor does not own the home and cannot be claimed exempt for that reason. If the trustee sues mother to avoid the transfer, the homestead exemption may not be claimed once the property is returned to the estate.

12. THE AUTOMATIC STAY IN CHAPTER 7 CASES

1. General

The filing of a petition in bankruptcy stops all creditors from attempting to collect any debt or to enforce any lien that existed on that date. Generally, it provides that a creditor may not "commence or continue any act" to collect a debt that existed when the bankruptcy was filed. Section 362(a) The stay has the force of an injunction and a violation can be punished with contempt and damages. It is effective even without actual notice.

2. Scope of the Stay

The automatic stay prohibits any act by any entity to commence or continue a judicial, administrative, or other action or proceeding *against the debtor* or *against property of the estate* that was or could have been commenced before the bankruptcy was filed. It prohibits a creditor from enforcing a judgment or lien or attempting to exercise control or possession of property of the estate. Section 362(a)

2.1 Purpose

The stay protects the property of the estate while the trustee investigates and decides whether there is anything to liquidate. The stay protects the debtor since the debt will be discharged and therefore cannot be enforced later.

2.2 Limitations

The stay does not prevent creditors from exercising any rights they may have beyond seizing property of the estate or chasing down the debtor. For example, suing guarantors or seizing property pledged by others is not stayed.

3. What the Stay Does Not Stop

There are many exceptions to the automatic stay, Section 362(b), including:

1) criminal actions. Section 362(b)(1)

2) actions to establish paternity; or to establish or modify alimony, maintenance, or support or child custody issues; or to collect alimony, maintenance, or support from property that is not property of the estate. Section 362(b)(2)

3) (A) an audit by a governmental unit to determine tax liability; (B) the issuance to the debtor by a governmental unit of a notice of tax deficiency; (C) a demand for tax returns. Section 362(b)(9)

4) the eviction of a tenant if the creditor obtained a judgment in an unlawful detainer action before the bankruptcy filing unless the debtor meets the requirements of Section 362(l) by showing a state court right to cure and thereby avoid the judgment. Section 362(b)(22)

4. Relief From the Stay

A creditor may file a motion with the court asking for relief from the stay, that is, the right to proceed with its remedies notwithstanding the filing of the bankruptcy. Relief from stay is fairly rare in chapter 7 cases and is limited to certain situations.

The code provides in Section 362(d) that a creditor must be granted relief by the court:

a) for cause;

b) for lack of adequate protection;

c) when the debtor has no equity in the property and the property is not needed for an effective reorganization.

4.1 Cause

Relief for cause, Section 362(d)(1), usually arises when the creditor desires to continue non bankruptcy court litigation notwithstanding the bankruptcy filing. Relief is granted only in a few specific fact situations. Most common is when the creditor is seeking to obtain a judgment against the debtor *solely* for the purpose of pursuing insurance owned by the debtor. Relief will be granted to permit the creditor to proceed with the litigation but not to collect any resulting judgment from the debtor. Another example is when the creditor is suing the debtor for something that will be non-dischargeable if the creditor is successful, or where the amount of the claims needs to be quantified and the burden on the debtor is not too great.

4.2 Lack of Adequate Protection

This arises only as to secured creditors. This basis for relief is uncommon in chapter 7 cases. The concept is that secured creditors should not have their positions eroded by the delay caused by the chapter 7 proceeding. If the secured creditor can establish that its collateral is decreasing in value, the court will require payments to the creditor by the debtor (if the debtor is opposing the motion) or the trustee equal to the erosion or will grant relief from stay and allow the creditor to foreclose.[58] Section 362(d)(1). Adequate protection is defined in Section 361. The trustee or the debtor has the burden of proof to show that the creditor is adequately protected. Section 362(g)(2)

4.3 No Equity and Not Needed for an Effective Reorganization

This is the typical motion for relief in chapter 7 cases. Section 362(d)(2) No equity means that the total liens on the property are greater than the value of the property. If there is no equity, a creditor seeking to foreclose must be granted relief. The trustee cannot generate funds for unsecured creditors since there is no equity and therefore there is no reason to delay the foreclosure

---

[58] *United Savings Assn v. Timbers of Inwood Forest*, 484 U.S. 365 (1988)(adequate protection required only when the property is decreasing in value)

sale. In a chapter 7, property is never needed for an effective reorganization since debtors do not reorganize in chapter 7. The creditor has the burden of proof to establish that there is no equity in the property. Section 362(g)(1) The creditor typically uses the debtor's schedules as evidence to establish that there is no equity.

5.   Procedure for Obtaining Relief From Stay

The creditor seeking relief from the automatic stay must file a motion and set it for hearing. The hearing usually takes place in about 30 days. The motion must be served on the chapter 7 trustee as well as the debtor and her counsel.

6.   Secured Creditors of Consumer Goods

The automatic stay is lifted as to a secured creditor with a lien on consumer goods if the debtor does not timely meet his obligations under Section 521(a)(2) to reaffirm the debt, redeem the property or return it to the creditor. Section 362(h)

7.   Duration of the Automatic Stay

7.1 As to the Debtor

As to the debtor, the automatic stay terminates when the discharge is entered. Section 362(c)(2) The discharge, of course, is an injunction itself ordering creditors to make no attempt to collect the debt forever. Section 524 Upon entry of the discharge, creditors with non-dischargeable debts may continue their collection efforts against the debtor and may seize property that is not property of the estate.

7.2 As to Property of the Estate

As to property of the estate, the automatic stay terminates as soon as the property is no longer property of the estate. Section 362(c)(1) The property is no longer property of the estate when it is abandoned by the trustee or the case is closed. Abandonment prior to the closing of the case requires notice and a court order.

8.   Violations of the Automatic Stay

8.1 Effect of Acts Which Violate the Stay

Acts taken in violation of the automatic stay are void.[59] If, for example, a secured creditor files a notice of default after the petition has been filed thus violating the automatic stay, the notice of default is void. It does not have to be set aside because it is without legal effect as a matter of law.

8.2 Penalties for Violation of the Stay

The code provides that any *individual* injured by a willful violation of the automatic stay "shall recover actual damages, including costs and attorney's fees, and, in appropriate circumstances, may recover punitive damages."[60] Section 362(k). Persons who unknowingly violate the stay are required to take positive steps to undo the violation such as return the asset to the estate [61] or give notice that the act has no effect.

8.3 Annulment of the Automatic Stay

The court is authorized to annul the stay or, in effect, grant relief retroactively thereby avoiding the rule that an act in violation of the stay is void. To annual the stay, the court usually must find that the creditor had no notice, or was actively deceived by the debtor and that relief would probably have been granted had it been requested.[62]

9.   The Automatic Stay in Subsequent Cases

If the debtor files a case which is subsequently dismissed, the automatic stay is limited in subsequent cases.

---

[59] *In re Schwartz*, 954 F.2d 569 (9th Cir. 1992)
[60] *In re Peralta*, 317 B.R. 381 (9th Cir. BAP 2004)(specific intent not required when determining willfulness); *In re Dawson*, 390 F.3d 1139 (9th Cir. 2004)(court may award damages for emotional distress for willful violations of the stay)
[61] *In re Abrams*, 127 B.R. 239 (9th Cir. BAP 1991)
[62] *In re National Environmental Waste Corp.*, 129 F.3d 1052 (9th Cir. 1997)

When a second case is filed within one year, the automatic stay with respect to secured creditors "terminates with respect to the debtor on the 30th day after the filing of the later case." Section 362(c)(3)(A) The debtor may file a motion for "continuation of the automatic stay" if the debtor "demonstrates that the filing of the later case is in good faith as to the creditors to be stayed." Section 362(c)(3)(B) The code sets forth in detail the factors to be considered when determining good faith. It is not clear whether or not this means a foreclosure sale may go forward automatically since the stay is lifted, by the terms of the code, "with respect to the debtor" and therefore apparently not as to property of the estate.

When a third case is filed within one year, the stay "shall not go into effect upon the filing of the later case."[63] Section 362(c)(4) The debtor may seek a stay by showing that the subsequent filings were "in good faith." Query what would happen if there were non-exempt equity in property which the trustee wanted to sell. It does not appear the trustee would be entitled to get the stay extended.

13.   THE TRUSTEE'S ABILITY TO EXPAND THE ESTATE: PREFERENCES

1.   General

Preferences are payments or other transfers made by the debtor to her creditors shortly before filing a petition. Preferences are unique to bankruptcy, that is, creditors cannot seek to avoid these transfers outside of bankruptcy.[64] Bankruptcy law gives the trustee the right to avoid preferences and thereby expand the estate, that is, recover property which will be subsequently distributed to the creditors.

---

[63] *In re Nelson*, 391 B.R. 437 (9th Cir. BAP, June 2008)(creditor may ignore third bankruptcy filed within one year)

[64] See Cal. C.C.P. 1800(b) which creates preference avoidance rights in an Assignment for the Benefit of Creditors. The Ninth Circuit has ruled that Section 1800(b) is unconstitutional in *Sherwood Partners v. Lycos, Inc.* 394 F.3d 1198 (9th Cir. Jan. 2005). The California Court of Appeals has begged to differ in *Haberbush v. Charles and Dorothy Cummins Family Ltd. Partnership*, 139 Cal.App.4th 1630 (Cal.App. 2 Dist. May 31, 2006)

Preference actions in individual chapter 7 cases are fairly rare. The issue arises typically in the pre-petition planning by the debtor when he discovers that he has property which may be seized by the chapter 7 trustee. He will want to put it out of the reach of the trustee before he files. If the debtor, for example, pays his mother a significant amount shortly before filing bankruptcy, the trustee will sue mother for return of the funds so that the funds may be distributed evenly to all creditors.

2.   Definition of a Preference

Preferences have seven (7) parts. Section 547(b). It must be a transfer of:

1) an interest in property,

2) of the debtor,

3) to or for the benefit of a creditor,

4) on account of an antecedent debt,

5) made within 90 days of the filing of the bankruptcy petition or within one year if the transfer is to an insider,

6) made while the debtor was insolvent,

7) which allows the creditor to receive more than he would have otherwise received in a chapter 7 proceeding.

2.1 Disclosure of Transfers

The forms that the debtor completes and files with the bankruptcy petition include a Statement of Financial Affairs which asks the consumer debtor to disclose all transfers of more than $600 in value outside of the ordinary course of business within the 90 days prior to the filing or within one year if the payment is made to an insider. The non-consumer debtor must disclose payments over $5,475.

2.2 Key Components

The key components of a preference are:

A Summary of Bankruptcy Law

a) a transfer of property of the debtor to a creditor. This includes payment of a debt with money or by a transfer of property to the creditor including a security interest. Thus if the debtor gives an unsecured creditor a security interest in his property (or if the creditor obtains a lien on the debtor's property involuntarily) and the other factors exist, the security interest can be avoided by the trustee as a preference. Payment by mother of the debtor's debt before he files is not a preference because the payment was not a transfer of the debtor's property.

b) antecedent debt. The transfer must pay an existing debt. A transfer for new consideration is not a preference. For example, the debtor buys a new suit the day before filing. The debtor pays a doctor several thousand dollars to perform an operation. The payment for the suit or the operation is not a preference because it was not made on account of an antecedent debt. The debtor received current consideration. Section 547(c)(1)

c) insolvency. The debtor must be insolvent when the transfer is made or become insolvent as a result of the transfer. Insolvency exists when the debtor's liabilities exceed his assets, i.e., a negative net worth. Section 101(31) The code presumes that the debtor was insolvent at the time of the transfer however this presumption may be rebutted. Section 547(f).

d) which gives the creditor more than he would have received in a chapter 7. This excludes nearly all transfers to secured creditors since the secured creditor would have received the entire collateral in the chapter 7 anyway and would sell it to collect the debt, whether or not there was a bankruptcy pending. Some transfers to secured creditors improve the position of the creditor and are therefore an avoidable preference. This requirement also excludes all transfers when the creditors are paid in full as part of the bankruptcy proceeding.

e) insiders. The code defines insiders as relatives (which is defined as "related by affinity or consanguinity within the third degree" including step or adoptive relationships), general partners, directors, officers, persons in control, managing agents and other such related individuals and entities. Section 101(31). These persons or entities are at much greater risk of having transfers to

77

them set aside since the lookback period is one year, not just ninety days.

2.3 Burden of Proof

The trustee has the burden of proof with respect to each of the components of a preference. Section 547(g)

3. Defenses

Some transfers which meet the seven requirements above are not preferences and cannot be avoided. They are:

a) payments made in the ordinary course of business. Section 547(c)(2) This is a common defense but is difficult to establish. The defendant in the action, that is, the transferee, must establish that the payment was in the ordinary course of his business as well as the business of the transferee. For example, if a baseball card store hires a painter to paint the store, the ordinary course defense would require a showing of when baseball card stores typically pay their bills and when painters typically collect. The defendant must examine the normal payment terms and processes of both industries to see if the exception applies.

b) payments made to the extent the creditor later gives new value. Section 547(c)(4) For example, the debtor makes an out-of-the-ordinary-course-of-business payment of $10,000 to a supplier on account of an antecedent debt within the preference period. Later, also within the preference period, the supplier ships an additional $8,000 worth of new merchandise. Only $2,000 of the original preference of $10,000 is avoidable by the trustee as the creditor provided "new value" to the debtor after receipt of the preference. New value is defined in Section 547(a)(2).

c) Payments made for alimony, child support etc may not be avoided by the trustee. Section 547(c)(7)

d) If the debtor's debts are primarily consumer debts, payments of $600 or less may not be avoided. Section 547(c)(8) If the debtor's debts are primarily business debts, payments of $5,475 or less may not be avoided. Section 547(c)(9)

3.3 Burden of Proof

The defendant has the burden of proof with respect to each of the above stated defenses. Section 547(g)

4. Preference Litigation

When the trustee determines that a preference has taken place, he commences an adversary proceeding against the recipient of the preference by filing a Complaint to Avoid Preference. The recipient/defendant is served and has 30 days or so to file an answer. All of the discovery rules apply and there can be depositions, Motions for Summary Judgment etc.[65] The end result is a trial and if the trustee wins he receives a judgment against the recipient which must be collected the same as any judgment. The defendant has the right to a jury unless he has filed a proof of claim.[66]

4.1 Preference Litigation is Not Common

Because recovery of a preference involves litigation which can be very expensive to the estate, preference litigation is rare and usually arises only when the preference is large, i.e., more than $10,000 or when the estate has significant funds to pay the costs of the litigation.

5. Standing to Bring a Preference Action

Only the trustee has standing to bring a preference avoidance action, Section 547(b), with one exception. When the property recovered would have been exempt had it not been transferred, and the transfer was involuntary, the debtor can bring the avoidance action provided the trustee "does not attempt to avoid such transfer." Section 522(h)

5.1 Example

Suppose a creditor garnishes the debtor's paycheck and collects $100 within 90 days of the bankruptcy filing. If the debtor could have exempted the $100, typically by using the wildcard

---

[65] Rule 7001
[66] *Schoenthal v. Irving Trust Co.*, 287 U.S. 92 (1932); *Katchen v. Landy*, 382 U.S. 323 (1966); *Langenkamp v. Culp*, 498 U.S. 42 (1990)

exemption, the debtor may file the preference action against the creditor if the trustee does not do so.

6. Statute of Limitations

The trustee must bring the action to avoid the preference within two years after the bankruptcy case is filed.[67] Section 546(a)

7. Disallowance of Claim for Failure to Repay a Preference

The claim of a creditor is disallowed if the creditor received a preference and has not returned the preference received to the estate. Section 502(d)

8. Comprehensive Example

John Allen sells jewelry. He files a chapter 7 bankruptcy petition on January 2, 2009. An analysis of his books for the one year period prior to January 2, 2009 discloses the following:

1) Payment to Vendor A of $15,000 on December 3, 2008;

2) Payment to Vendor B of $3,000 on October 1, 2008;

3) Payment to Vendor C of $6,000 on March 1, 2008. Vendor C is owned by John's mother;

4) Payments were made on a loan secured by a truck for each of the 12 months;

5) Twelve mortgage payments were made to the bank which holds a first deed of trust on John's home. All of the payments were late;

6) On June 19, 2008 a payment of $5,000 was made to Vendor D and 30 days later another payment of $5,000. The entire amount was due in the ordinary course of business on June 19, 2008. Vendor D is now out of business itself.

---

[67] *Bailey v. Glover,* 88 U.S. 342 (1874)(the two year statute is tolled if the debtor actively conceals the transfer from the trustee)

7) On September 17, 2008, Vendor E was paid $17,000 to pay off an old debt. The next day, Vendor E shipped $11,000 in additional goods to John on open account;

8) On December 12, 2008, Vendor F sued John for the $100,000 it was owed at the time. To settle the suit, John gave Vendor F a lien on his home.

9) On December 5, 2008, John transferred a vacant lot he owned to his brother for no consideration.

10) On December 6, 2008, John transferred a condo he owned in Vail, Colorado to an unhappy customer who was threatening to sue John. The customer then dropped its threats.

8.1 Analysis

What are the legal effects of these transactions if any?

1) The payment to Vendor A is a preference unless it was made in the ordinary course of business. The trustee would sue Vendor A and demand repayment of the $15,000 to the estate. If Vendor A had an outstanding claim against the debtor on the petition date, the claim would be disallowed unless and until Vendor A returns the $15,000 to the estate.

2) The payment to Vendor B is not a preference because it was made beyond the 90 day boundary.

3) The payment to Vendor C is a preference because it was made to an insider within one year of filing bankruptcy. Again, it would not be a preference if it was made in the ordinary course of business (or if the debtor was not insolvent at the time of the payment).

4) Payments to secured creditors are not preferences because the payment does not give the creditor more than it would have received in a chapter 7, i.e., it would have received the payments or the truck in either case.

5) Same answer as 4. The fact that the payments are late is irrelevant.

6) The first payment to Vendor D is not a preference but the second payment is since it was not in the ordinary course of business. Since Vendor D has gone out of business, there is not much point in pursuing the preference action since it will probably not result in any new funds to the estate anyway.

7) Vendor E did not receive a preference because the payment was beyond the 90 day period. If Vendor E is an insider and therefore the payment is otherwise a preference, the preference is reduced by the subsequent delivery of goods (the "new value") of $11,000.

8) This is a preference. The transfer of a lien during the preference period will allow Vendor F to be paid in full which is more than it would have received in a chapter 7.

9) This is not a preference because the transfer was not on account of an antecedent debt. If anything, it is a fraudulent conveyance because it was transferred for less than fair value.

10) This transfer is a preference. To the extent the value of the condo was more than the claim, it is also a fraudulent conveyance.

14.   THE TRUSTEE'S ABILITY TO EXPAND THE ESTATE: FRAUDULENT CONVEYANCES

1.   General

A fraudulent conveyance is a transfer of property made by the debtor before the bankruptcy filing either for less than fair value or with actual intent to delay, hinder or defraud creditors. Typically it comes up when the debtor discovers that he will lose the property to the trustee in chapter 7. He then transfers the property to an insider or in a transaction designed to either avoid discovery or to mislead the trustee as to the true owner.[68] The fraudulent conveyance may be set aside by the trustee, that is, "avoided." The transferee must return the asset transferred to him or it or return the fair value to the estate. Section 548(a)(1)

---

[68] *Dean v. Davis*, 242 U.S. 438 (1917)(transfer of lien to brother-in-law is a fraudulent conveyance)

Unlike preferences, fraudulent conveyances exist both under the bankruptcy code, Section 548, and under state law.[69] These transfers may be avoided by creditors if no bankruptcy proceeding exists. The bankruptcy code specifically gives the trustee the power to avoid many kinds of these transfers and the "strong arm clause" gives the trustee the right to use state law to avoid these and other transfers. Section 544

2.   Definition

Fraudulent conveyances under the Bankruptcy Code are transfers made by the debtor within two years[70] prior to the bankruptcy filing: Section 548

a) with actual intent to delay, hinder or defraud any creditor; or

b) made for less than reasonably equivalent value when:

i) the debtor was insolvent, or

ii) the transfer caused the debtor to become insolvent, or

iii) the transfer left the debtor without enough assets to reasonably continue to conduct his business, or

iv) the debtor incurred debts that he reasonably believed was beyond his ability to repay.

2.1 Disclosure

The forms that the debtor completes and files with the bankruptcy petition include a Statement of Financial Affairs which requires the debtor to disclose any transfer of property within the past two years. The trustee often asks the debtor at the meeting of creditors whether he or she has transferred property within the past five years.

---

[69] In California see Civil Code 3439
[70] Under California Law, the statute of limitations to avoid a fraudulent conveyance is four years from the date of discovery of the transfer but in no event more than six years after the transfer. Cal. Civil Code Section 3439.09.

2.2 Non-Disclosure

The consequences of being less than fully truthful on the schedules are that the debtor could be charged with bankruptcy fraud and face a jail sentence[71] and/or the debtor could face losing his discharge for making a false oath. Section 727(a).

2.3 Example

Assume that the debtor transfers his home by deed to his mother for no consideration one year (or one month or one day) prior to filing bankruptcy. If the transfer was made with actual intent to hinder, delay or defraud his creditors, it may be avoided as a fraudulent conveyance. If the debtor's actual intent is unclear, the transfer still may be avoided since the transfer was made for less than fair consideration (provided the transfer left the debtor insolvent). If the transfer was in payment of a debt owed to mother and was within one year of the filing of the bankruptcy, it is a preference.

2.4 Fraud Not Required

It is important to be aware that a fraudulent conveyance does not require fraud. Indeed the parties could be absolutely in good faith and disclose every conceivable aspect of the transaction to each other, and all of the debtor's creditors for that matter. If however the transfer was for less than fair value, it is at risk. For example, if the debtor sells his boat to a dealer for less than fair value but in good faith, the transfer may be set aside as a fraudulent conveyance.

2.5 "Badges of Fraud"

Determination of the "actual intent" of the debtor at the time of the transfer can be problematic. This has led to use of the "badges of fraud"[72] sometimes called the "smell test," i.e., does it stink? Badges of fraud include a transfer to an insider; a transfer when the debtor retains possession; a transfer at or near the time

---

[71] 18 U.S.C. 151 et seq
[72] See Cal. Civ. Code Section 3439.04(b) for a complete list.

when a debtor has been sued; a transfer of substantially all of the debtor's assets; a transfer which leaves the debtor insolvent.

2.6 Protection for the Buyer-Transferee

When the transferee has paid value which the court later determines is less than fair value, the transferee receives a lien on the property returned for the value paid provided the transferee was "in good faith," meaning not part of a scheme by the debtor to hide property from his creditors. Section 548(c)

2.7 Insolvency

Insolvency is defined in the bankruptcy code. Section 101(31)[73] In general, "balance sheet" insolvency exists where the debts exceed the non exempt assets of the debtor. Another generally accepted definition is "cash flow" insolvency where the debtor is not generally paying his debts as they become due.

3.   Strong-Arm Clause

The bankruptcy code gives the Trustee a status at the outset of the case which helps him administer the case. Specifically he is said to be a hypothetical lien creditor as of the date of filing, whether or not one actually exists; a creditor with an unsatisfied execution as of the date of filing; a bona fide purchaser of real property who has perfected his transfer at the time of filing; and, a creditor who holds an unsecured claim and has the right under state law to avoid transfers or obligations of the debtor. Section 544

3.1 Purpose

The purpose of the strong arm clause is to allow the trustee to avoid transfers using state law which often gives special rights to these types of creditors.

3.1.1 Example One

In California, a lien creditor is given priority over unperfected security interests. These are so called "hidden

---

[73] In California see Civ. Code Section 3439.02

liens" where a document purports to give a creditor a lien but such interest has not been perfected because the parties agreed to hide the security interest from other creditors or potential creditors (or some other reason). The trustee is given the status of a lien creditor so that he may bring an action in his own name, as trustee of the estate, under state law in state court or in bankruptcy court to avoid the hidden lien.

3.1.2 Example Two

A hidden transfer of real property by Quitclaim or other deed, that is an unrecorded deed, may be avoided by a subsequent bona fide purchaser under state law. That status is given to the trustee whether or not such a bona fide purchaser really exists. Section 544(a)(3)   Again the trustee will file suit against the transferee to set aside the unrecorded deed thus making more assets available to general creditors.

4.   The "Lookback" Period for Avoidance of Fraudulent Conveyances

Under the bankruptcy code, the improper transfer must have occurred within two years of the date of the filing of the petition. Section 548(a)(1) Under California law, the transfer may be avoided if it was made within four years before the bankruptcy filing or within seven years before the filing if the transfer could not have been discovered within the seven years through ordinary diligence.[74]

5.   Statute of Limitations

As with preferences, the trustee must file a complaint to avoid the transfer which commences an adversary proceeding.[75] The defendant has the right to trial by jury unless he has filed a proof of claim.[76] The trustee must bring the action to avoid the fraudulent conveyance, that is file a

---

[74] Cal. Civil Code Section 3439.09.

[75] Rule 7001.

[76] *Granfinanciera, S.A. v. Norberg,* 492 U.S. 33 (1989)(right to a jury not changed under the new bankruptcy code); *Katchen v. Landy,* 382 U.S. 323 (1966); *Langenkamp v. Culp,* 498 U.S. 42 (1990)

complaint in bankruptcy court or state court, within two years after the bankruptcy case is filed.[77] Section 546(a)

6.   Comprehensive Examples

David Debtor files a chapter 7 petition on October 7, 2008. The chapter 7 trustee, after reviewing the books and records of the debtor, finds the following:

1) On March 15, 2008, the debtor transferred title to his Mercedes to his mother. He retained possession of the auto.

2) In 2008, the debtor started a college savings account for his child by putting $10,000 into a bank account entitled "David Debtor as trustee for Child Debtor."

3) In 2008, the debtor obtained a loan from Finance Company for $35,000. As part of the loan he gave Finance Company a first deed of trust on his home.

4) In February, 2008, the debtor gave his son a third deed of trust on his home to secure a loan he had received from his son one year earlier.

5) In May, 2008, the debtor borrowed $50,000 from his mother. He gave her a fourth deed of trust on his home at the time of the loan however he did not record it for one month.

6) In June, 2008, the debtor guaranteed an automobile loan for an auto purchased by his daughter.

7) In July, 2008, the debtor's father-in-law paid a debt owed by the debtor which the father-in-law had guaranteed.

6.1 Analysis

1) If the debtor did not receive "fair value" for the auto, the transfer is a fraudulent conveyance and the trustee will sue mother for an order requiring her to return the auto or its value to the estate. The

---

[77] *Bailey v. Glover*, 88 U.S. 342 (1874)(Two year statute is tolled when the debtor conceals the transfer from the trustee)

trustee may proceed under Section 548 of the bankruptcy code or under state law using Section 544. The fact that the debtor retained possession is admissible evidence of actual intent to hide assets from his creditors but does not prove that by itself. The debtor will not be able to exempt the automobile after it is returned to the estate. Section 522(g) Mother will receive a lien in the vehicle for any actual consideration she paid provided she can establish good faith which seems unlikely.

2) A gift, by definition, is a transfer for no value and on that basis is a fraudulent conveyance however it is not avoidable unless the debtor was insolvent at the time of the transfer or the transfer caused him to become insolvent.

3) This is not an avoidable transfer because the debtor received fair value, i.e., money for the transfer of the security interest.

4) This is not a fraudulent transfer because the debtor received value even if it was one year earlier. On the other hand, it could be a fraudulent transfer if the transfer was made with actual intent to delay, hinder or harass creditors. Irrespective, it is avoidable as a preference because it is a transfer to an insider on account of an antecedent debt within one year of filing bankruptcy. Section 547(b)(4)(B)

5) Again, this is not a fraudulent conveyance because the debtor received fair value however, it is a preference because the trust deed became effective only when recorded. Since it was recorded one month after the proceeds were received, the transfer is deemed to have taken place at that time and is therefore "on account of an antecedent debt."

6) This is an avoidable transaction, that is, the trustee will not have to pay the debt if the guarantee caused the debtor to become insolvent.

7)   This is neither a preference nor a fraudulent conveyance in the debtor's case. The transfer by father-in-law was not a transfer of funds of the debtor. The fact that it wiped out a debt of the debtor does not matter. It would be a fraudulent conveyance if the father-in-law filed his own case since it is a transfer with nothing received in return.

15. SECURED CREDITORS – AN OVERVIEW

1. General

Secured creditors are creditors that have a lien on property, sometimes said to be the creditor's collateral. The term "lien" is the same as "security interest." This lien is said to "attach" to the collateral. When the creditor has collateral (or a lien [or security interest]) in some particular property, the creditor is "secured" *by that property*. Outside of bankruptcy, the debt can be enforced by seizing the collateral and selling it. Furthermore, if an unsecured judgment creditor seizes another creditor's collateral, the secured creditor's lien remains attached and must be paid first when the property is sold. If the property is sold or otherwise transferred by its owner, the lien usually remains attached.

1.1 Example One

Bank loans debtor $10,000 to buy a car. The bank retains a lien on the car as part of the transaction. If the debtor misses any payments, the bank may seize the car and sell it without court action being required. Another creditor, a credit card company for example, cannot seize the car without a court order or a judgment. That creditor must then sell it through a Sheriff's sale and the proceeds of the sale must go first to the bank until they are paid in full and then to the credit card company.

1.2 Example Two

If a debtor owns a car subject to Bank's lien and transfers title to his mother, even for value, the lien remains attached to the car and is otherwise unaffected by the transfer, i.e., if the payments are not made, Bank may repossess and sell the car.

2. Types of Liens

Liens are either consensual or non-consensual. Consensual, or voluntary liens, are those which are created and attach through the agreement of the creditor and the borrower (debtor). Non-consensual liens attach by law, without the consent of the owner of the property.

2.1 Consensual Liens on Real Property

A consensual security interest or lien in real property is created by a deed of trust. The deed of trust describes the property (which usually includes any rental income and insurance proceeds) and many of the rights of the creditor. This area of law is heavily statutory and most of the secured creditor's rights and duties are circumscribed by statute.[78] The creditor must follow these statutes when enforcing its default rights under the deed of trust to seize the property.

For example, upon the occurrence of a default, the lender, through the trustee named in the Deed of Trust, must record and serve a Notice of Default giving the property owner a period of time to cure or "fix" the default. After this cure period, the lender must again give Notice of Sale and have a public auction to assure that the property is sold at its highest value. Any funds remaining after all lienholders are paid is paid over to the property owner.

2.2 Consenual Liens on Personal Property

To have a consensual security interest in personal property, the creditor must generally have a written agreement which is properly perfected.[79] The written agreement must describe the debtor and the collateral. It usually also establishes the secured creditor's rights to seize and sell the collateral although again, this area is heavily statutory. A written agreement is not required when the secured creditor takes physical possession of the collateral.

Perfection of the security interest is usually accomplished by filing a Form UCC 1 with the Secretary of State. This UCC 1 describes the debtor, the creditor and the collateral. The purpose of perfection is to give notice to subsequent buyers or lenders of the existence of a security agreement and therefore a lien on the property. An unperfected security interest is enforceable by the creditor against the debtor but does not have priority over other creditors to whom perfection is improper.

---

[78] In California, see Cal. Civil Code Section 2924 et seq.
[79] In California, See Cal. Commercial Code Section 9203 et seq.

3. Non-Consensual Liens

There are many federal and state statutes that give entities a security interest in certain specified assets of the debtor.

The Internal Revenue Code gives the I.R.S. a lien on all property of the debtor when the debtor refuses to pay a tax that has been assessed against him.[80] The lien must be recorded in the county where the assets are located to have priority over secured creditors who perfect their security interest after the I.R.S. lien arises.[81]

Judgment liens attach to all real property located in the county where the abstract of judgment is recorded.[82] This lien has priority over all liens perfected after the recording of the abstract.

Other common non consensual liens are mechanics liens,[83] repairman's liens, warehouseman's liens and landlord's liens.

The creditors who hold these involuntary liens are secured creditors who have all of the rights in bankruptcy of secured creditors to adequate protection and to priority over all other creditors (except those with senior liens on the same assets).

4. Priorities Among Secured Creditors

When more than one creditor has a security interest in the same collateral, there is a priority "pecking" order. The creditor who has a first priority lien can enforce its lien generally without regard to junior secured creditors. When the senior lienholder seizes and sells the property, the buyer will take it with no liens attached, in other words, the seizure and sale will "wipe out" the junior lienholders. Junior lienholders are in a more precarious position but they knew they were junior when they advanced the loan or credit and took the risk of losing the collateral to the senior lienholder. In fact, they probably charged a higher rate of interest to cover their increased risk.

---

[80] 26 U.S.C. 6321
[81] 26 U.S.C. 6323(f)
[82] Cal Code of Civil Procedure 697.320.
[83] Cal Civil Code Section 3110 et seq.

The creditor who has second priority can enforce its lien however enforcement will not affect the senior lienholder. If the second priority creditor seizes the collateral and sells it, the senior lienholder's lien will remain attached to the property after the sale unless paid.

Priority is determined generally by the time of perfection, that is, the first to perfect has superior rights over all who perfect later. A major exception to this rule of first to perfect has first priority is the purchase money security interest. When the lender (or seller) advances the funds so that the debtor can buy the asset, the lender's security interest will have first priority over everyone if the lender perfects his interest within ten days after the debtor takes possession of the collateral.

5. Real Property Foreclosure Sales

Suppose the debtor's home has liens as follows:

Fair Market Value	$200,000	Date of Notice of Default
First Trust Deed	80,000	2/1/09
Second Trust Deed	100,000	3/1/09
Third Trust Deed	50,000	4/1/09

The homeowner is behind on her payments to all three creditors and each have filed a Notice of Default (NOD) on the date stated above. The foreclosure sale dates of each TD holder will be about four months after the NOD date. If the first TD has its sale on 6/1/09 or thereabouts, the liens of the junior lienholders will be wiped out, that is, the buyer (the successful bidder) will receive title to the property without the other liens attached. The junior lienholders will therefore typically appear at the sale and bid. The minimum bid will be $80,000 since that is what the first will bid. Rather than pay $80,000 at the sale, the second will probably "cure," that is, pay the first lienholder the amount that is in default prior to the sale. The sale will then be stopped because there is no longer any default.

The second will then have its sale on or about 7/1/09. The sale will wipe out the lien of the third, i.e., junior to the selling lienholder, but not of the first. The second will bid the amount it is owed, $100,000 and if it is the successful bidder, it will own the property subject to the first. Contrary to common belief, the bidder does not have to bid enough to pay off the first. It is unlikely that the third will cure the second or bid at the sale since there is so little equity considering the first lienholder will remain and $100,000 will have to be paid to the second.

6. Deficiency Judgments

Under California law, a secured creditor who has a lien on real property generally cannot obtain a deficiency judgment against the borrower after that creditor conducts a foreclosure sale.[84] If the creditor wants to obtain a deficiency judgment against the borrower, the creditor has to foreclose judicially, that is, file a lawsuit and ask the court to oversee the foreclosure sale.

A secured creditor who has had his lien wiped out by the foreclosure sale of a senior lienholder can sue on the promissory note.

A secured creditor whose lien is on personal property can sue for a deficiency judgment after selling the collateral.

7. Leases

Traditionally a lease is a transfer by an owner of possession of an asset to a user. The user pays a price for the period of time of his use and then returns the assets to its owner.[85]

It is common today for a sales transaction to be structured as if it were a lease when, in reality, it is a conditional sale or, more properly, a sale with the seller retaining a security interest in the asset as security for payment of the purchase price.

Whether the transaction is a lease or a sale/security interest is of major importance in a bankruptcy proceeding. If it is a sale/security interest transaction, it must be properly perfected to be enforceable against the trustee. If it is a lease, it is an executory contract that the debtor or trustee may not assume without curing all defaults. Section 365.

Whether a transaction is really a lease or a disguised sale/security interest depends on the intent of the parties. This intent is determined by studying the "four corners" of the transaction. For example, if the buy out

---

[84] Cal. Civil Code Section 580(b)
[85] Cal. Commercial Code Section 10101 et seq.

price at the end of the lease term is nominal or is such that the lessee would have no alternative but to exercise the option, it is almost surely a sale. If the term of the lease spans most of the anticipated life of the asset, it is probably a sale. If the total of the lease payments and buy out price computes out to the purchase price of the asset plus a commercially reasonable interest rate, it is probably a sale. Of course, combinations of these factors could establish the nature of the transaction as a sale.

Lessors should perfect their position by filing a UCC 1 immediately after the transaction has been completed. If the transaction is characterized as a secured transaction, the creditor (lessor) will be required to comply with Article 9 of the Uniform Commercial Code not only as to perfection, but as to seizure rights, notice and disposition of the proceeds irrespective of the terms of the lease.

8. Secured Creditors in Chapter 7 Bankruptcy Cases

8.1 General

The rights of secured creditors, consensual or otherwise, are generally not changed in chapter 7 except that the secured creditor is prevented from exercising its right to seize the collateral until it secures permission from the bankruptcy court or the case ends. The loan agreement, including the interest rate and due date, may be revised in Chapter 11 and 13 unless the collateral is the residence of the debtor or certain auto and personal property loans. Section 1129(a) and Section 1322(b)

8.2 Amount of the Secured Creditor's Claim

The secured creditor's claim (or the amount owed to it) is fixed as of the date of the filing of the bankruptcy petition, the same as all other creditors. Section 502(b) The claim, as of the filing date, includes late charges, attorney's fees, advances for taxes, insurance etc. Whatever is provided for in the agreement and has accrued as of the filing date.

Oversecured creditors, i.e. where the value of the collateral is more than the creditor's claim, are allowed postpetition interest, attorney's fees, and other expenses provided for in the agreement up to the value of the security (or until they are no longer oversecured). Section 506(b) This issue would arise when the trustee wants to sell property subject to a lien. The trustee must pay the oversecured creditor the amount owed including interest, attorneys fees and costs up to the time of the payment.

A non consensual oversecured creditor, i.e., the IRS, is allowed postpetition interest but not fees and costs since there is no agreement.[86]

9. Undersecured Creditors

When the value of the collateral is less than the amount owed to the secured creditor, the creditor is "undersecured." Section 506(a) Suppose the debtor owes his bank $50,000 secured by his inventory. If the inventory is only worth $35,000, the bank is undersecured. If the secured creditor seizes the inventory and sells it, a deficiency of $15,000 will still be owed although the debt will be discharged in bankruptcy. This particular creditor is really only secured as to $35,000 and is unsecured as to the remaining $15,000.

As we have stated at length, bankruptcy does not really change the status of the undersecured creditor. His right to seize the collateral is stayed. As to the deficiency, he will share pro-rata along with the rest of the unsecured creditors. The lien on the collateral remains with a few exceptions and when the case is over, if the chapter 7 trustee has not sold the asset, the creditor is free to pursue it although he cannot pursue the debtor for the deficiency if the debtor has been granted a discharge.

16. TREATMENT OF SECURED DEBTS IN CHAPTER 7: REAFFIRMATION, REDEMPTION OR RETURN

1. General

It is important to distinguish between debts and liens. A debt is an obligation to pay money to a creditor. It is enforced typically by suit seeking a judgment against the obligor for damages. A lien on property gives the creditor the right to seize the specific piece of property and sell it

---

[86] *U.S. v. Ron Pair Enterprises, Inc.* 489 U.S. 235 (1989)

to collect the debt. No suit is required. *Debts* are discharged – the creditor may no longer sue the debtor to collect the debt. *Liens* survive the bankruptcy – the creditor may seize its collateral after the bankruptcy and sell it to collect all or a portion of the debt irrespective of the discharge granted to the debtor.

Property of the estate which is subject to a creditor's lien may be sold by the trustee only if there is *equity* over and above the amount of the claimed exemption. If there is no equity, or the equity is exempt, the trustee will abandon the property back to the debtor, Section 554, who will then have to deal with the secured creditor's lien if he wants to keep the property.

2.   When There is No Non-Exempt Equity in the Property

If property which is a creditor's collateral has sufficient non-exempt equity, the trustee will sell it, pay the secured debt as part of the sale and retain the remainder above the exemption. When the property is to be abandoned by the trustee because there is no non-exempt equity, the debtor must make a choice regarding the property. He can *return* the asset to the secured creditor; *reaffirm* the debt; *redeem* the asset; or in some cases, simply continue to pay the debt until it is paid in full, the so-called "ride-through." He must however choose one of those options before the case ends.

2.1   Statement of Intentions

One of the forms the debtor is required to file in a chapter 7 bankruptcy case is called a Statement of Intentions. This statement advises the secured creditors whether the debtor intends to return, reaffirm, redeem or simply continue paying the debt. Section 521(a)(2)(A) This Statement of Intention must be filed by the Debtor within 15 days after the petition is filed and the intention must be performed within 30 days of the meeting of creditors.

2.2   Return

When this is the debtor's choice, the creditor picks up the asset and that is the end of the matter; the debt is discharged. The creditor must wait until the case is over to pick up the asset or obtain relief from stay to do it earlier.

2.3 Reaffirm

When this is the choice, the debtor executes a new agreement with the creditor which must be approved by the court before it is enforceable. This "resurrects the debt" which makes it enforceable against the debtor personally in the future notwithstanding the discharge. Section 524(c)

2.4 Redeem

When this is the debtor's choice, the debtor may pay the creditor the current value of the asset. Redemption removes the lien and the previous debt is discharged. The parties must agree on the value or ask the court to set the value. The debt must be paid in a single payment unless, of course, the parties agree to something else.[87] Section 722

2.5 Continue Making the Payments, the "Ride-Through"

In some cases, the debtor may simply continue making the payments according to the original agreement. As long as there is no default, the creditor cannot enforce its rights. When the payments are completed, the lien is gone. This choice is sometimes known as the "ride-through," i.e., no additional action is taken by either the debtor or the creditor. The debtor simply continues making the monthly payments. The most common "ride-through" is mortgage loans. The debtor is not required to reaffirm loans secured by real property. Section 524 He simply keeps making the payments as required by the promissory note. If the debtor misses a payment in the future, the mortgage lender may begin foreclosure but may not sue on the loan because it has been discharged.[88]

3. Purchase Money Loans Secured by Personal Property

The 2005 Amendments provide that the debtor *must reaffirm* purchase money loans secured by personal property, or redeem or return

---

[87] There are lenders who will provide the funds to redeem assets. These new loans are typically quite expensive as can be imagined.

[88] The mortgage lender probably has no rights to a deficiency anyway under state law. See Cal. Civil Code Section 580(a) et seq

the property within 45 days after the first meeting of creditors. Section 521(a)(6). This requirement had the greatest effect in the area of auto loans. Prior to 2005, the debtor typically simply continued to make the payments, i.e., the "ride-through," and as long as there was no default, the lender could do nothing. Reaffirmations were rare. Today, if the debtor does not reaffirm, redeem or return, the lender is granted relief from the automatic stay and may immediately repossess the property after the 45 days to perform the debtor's intention has expired. Section 521(a)(6)

4. Reaffirmation

Reaffirmation is a cumbersome process. A debt is never reaffirmed unless the court enters an order approving the reaffirmation. Section 524(c) Even then, the debtor may change her mind for 60 days after the order is entered. Section 524(c)(4) There are numerous and specific disclosures which must be made to the debtor before the reaffirmation can be approved. These disclosures are set forth specifically in the code. Section 524(k) The effect of reaffirmation is to resurrect the debt. It is no longer discharged. If it is not paid, the debtor may be sued and her assets seized after bankruptcy.

4.1 Procedure

Reaffirmation does not come easy for obvious reasons. Creditors strongly prefer reaffirmation and if it were easy, the debtor would be bombarded with requests, threats and demands. The code provides that no reaffirmation is effective unless the court holds a hearing attended by the debtor and informs the debtor of the ramifications of the reaffirmation and makes a determination that the reaffirmation is in the debtor's best interests, i.e., does not create a hardship on the debtor. Section 524(c)(3) Judges commonly deny theses requests. This hearing can be avoided if the debtor's attorney signs a statement declaring that the attorney has informed the debtor of the consequences and that the agreement "does not impose an undue hardship on the debtor." Section 524(c)(6)

4.2 Procedure on Mortgages

No hearing is required when the debt is "a consumer debt secured by real property." Section 524(c)(6)(B) Reaffirmation of mortgages is very rare and occurs usually when the lender is offering significant concessions in the mortgage.

4.3 Attorney Statements in Reaffirmation Procedure

Many attorneys will not execute the attorney statement for the reason that they simply cannot attest that the reaffirmation will not impose a hardship on the debtor. When this is the case, a hearing is required.

4.4 Negotiating the Reaffirmation

Typically the lender reviews the Debtor's Statement of Intention and contacts counsel to confirm the intent to reaffirm. The lender then prepares the forms including all the disclosures required and the Motion to the Court and sends it all to counsel. The debtor and/or his counsel should seek concessions from the lender as part of the reaffirmation such as a reduction in the interest rate and curing of defaults. Often debtors are afraid to ask for the concessions worrying that the creditor or the court will require them to return the property. Auto lenders especially prefer a reaffirmation to a repossession and should be pushed to give concessions to the debtor in exchange for the reaffirmation.

4.5 Auto Lenders

In the Central District of California, many auto lenders, although not all, have been repossessing the vehicle, even where there is no default on the loan, when there is no timely reaffirmation.[89]

4.6 Reaffirmation Deadlines

The reaffirmation agreement must be "made" before the discharge is entered. Section 524(c)(1)

---

[89] *In re Dumont*, 383 B.R. 481 (9th Cir. BAP, Feb, 2008)(confirming that the lender may repossess the vehicle even if there is no default where the debtor has not timely reaffirmed)

5. No "Strip Down" in Chapter 7

The lien which attaches to an asset may not be "stripped down" in a chapter 7.[90] Suppose the debtor owns a boat worth $20,000 on which he owes $30,000. The creditor's lien of $30,000 cannot be "stripped down" to $20,000 in a chapter 7. In other words, the debtor must pay the full amount of the lien according to its original terms in order to keep the asset.

17. UNSECURED CREDITORS IN CHAPTER 7 CASES

1.   General

Creditors, whether secured or not, are said to have a "claim" against the estate. A claim is considerably more broad than merely a debt.[91] The concept of claim is very important in bankruptcy because only claims are discharged, only claims will share in the distribution by the trustee if any, and only the collection of prepetition claims are stopped by the automatic stay.

1.1 Definition

Claim is defined in the code as a "... right to payment, whether or not such right is reduced to judgment, liquidated, unliquidated, fixed, contingent, matured, unmatured, disputed, undisputed, legal, equitable, secured or unsecured...". Section 101(5)(A). Debt is defined as "...liability on a claim." Section 101(12). Creditor is defined as an "...entity that has a claim against the debtor..." Section 101(10)(A).

1.2 Example One

Suppose the debtor is involved in an automobile accident which he admits was his fault shortly before filing a bankruptcy chapter. It does not matter whether or not a lawsuit has been

---

[90] *Dewsnup v. Timm*, 502 U.S. 410 (1992)

[91] *Williams v. U.S. Fidelity & Guaranty Company*, 236 U.S. 549 (1915)(surety company which posted a bond for the debtor has a claim against the debtor even though it had not paid on the bond when the bankruptcy was filed)

formally started or completed by entry of judgment against the debtor. Indeed the accident could have happened an hour before the filing. Either way a claim exists because the victim has a right to payment as of the filing date. The claim is discharged unless the claimant is successful in having the claim declared non-dischargeable. Section 523(a) or Section 727(a). Either way the claimant is stopped from proceeding in state court by the automatic stay, even if he simply wants to proceed against the debtor's insurance.

The claimant, i.e., creditor, can file a proof of claim with the bankruptcy clerk and share in the distribution of assets if there are any to distribute. Section 501 If he has obtained a state court judgment, that will establish the amount of the claim. If he has not yet obtained a judgment, he will simply estimate his claim. The claim is automatically "allowed" unless the debtor, the trustee or any party in interest objects. Section 502(a). If someone objects, the amount of the claim will be determined in a proceeding similar to usual litigation.[92]

1.3 Example Two

Suppose mother guarantees junior's car payment. If junior is current on the loan when mother files bankruptcy, her contingent obligation to the bank is nevertheless a claim of the bank and her obligation to the bank is discharged.

1.4 Example Three

Suppose an attorney has committed malpractice but his client does not realize it yet. Perhaps the attorney does not realize it either. Suppose he wrote a will improperly. The client has not yet passed on and therefore the family does not know of the mistake. The family has a claim against the lawyer and if the lawyer files bankruptcy, the contingent claim will be discharged unless an exception to discharge under Section 523(a) applies.[93]

---

[92] Rule 3007

[93] *In re Edge*, 60 B.R. 690 (Bkrtcy M.D. Tenn 1986)(undiscovered malpractice by dentist is discharged)

2.   Allowance of a Claim

A claim is "allowed" or "disallowed." Allowed means that the claimant will share in the distribution of the estate pro rata depending on how much there is to distribute and the total amount of allowed claims. Disallowed means the claimant gets nothing from the estate. In chapter 7s, the filing of a proof of claim form is required. If no one objects to the proof of claim, it is allowed. Section 502(a). A proof of claim may be filed by the claimant, Section 501; by the debtor, by the trustee[94] or by a co obligor of the debtor.[95]

2.1 Pre-Bankruptcy Litigation

A judgment entered by a court with competent jurisdiction cannot be attacked in bankruptcy court.[96]

3.   Deadline to File a Proof of Claim

If there appears to be no assets to distribute in the case, the notice of the filing of the bankruptcy petition sent to creditors by the court clerk will instruct creditors not to file proofs of claim until they are further notified.[97] Otherwise, the due date for filing the proof of claim in a chapter 7 case is 90 days after the first date set for the first meeting of creditors.[98] In Los Angeles, nearly all notices in Chapter 7 cases instruct the creditor not to file a proof of claim until the creditor is further notified. If the trustee determines that there will be or may be a distribution to creditors, he will ask the court clerk to send out a notice to creditors instructing them to file proofs of claim by a certain date.

3.1 Late Filed Proofs of Claim

A late filed proof of claim is not automatically disallowed. In fact, it will be paid if there are funds available after all other timely filed claims have been paid. Section 726(a)(2)

---

[94] Rule 3004   The debtor may wish to file a proof of claim for the IRS or an ex-wife, for example, to make sure they receive some of the distribution from the trustee.

[95] Rule 3005

[96] *Heiser v. Woodruff*, 327 U.S. 726 (1946)

[97] Rule 3002(c)(5)

[98] Rule 3002(c)

4.   Objections to Claims

Objections to claims in chapter 7 cases are rare. Unless the trustee has generated funds to distribute to unsecured creditors, it really does not matter how much any particular claim is. The claims are discharged irrespective of how much the creditor thinks it is owed.

When there are funds to distribute, typically the trustee will object to claims by filing a written objection with the bankruptcy court. There are eight substantive grounds to object: Section 502(b)

1) The claim is unenforceable either under state or federal law or under the terms of the agreement under which the claim is based.

2) The claim is for unmatured interest.

3) The claim is for property taxes which exceed the value of the property.

4) The claim is for the services of an insider or an attorney to the extent the claim is unreasonable.

5) The claim is for a debt that is unmatured and will not be discharged under Section 523.

6) If the claim is that of a lessor, it cannot exceed the greater of one years rent or 15% of the lease, not to exceed three years rent.

7) If the claim is by an employee based on damages for wrongful discharge, it cannot exceed one years compensation.

8) Relates to employment taxes.

4.1   Objections to Claims on Procedural Grounds

The proof of claim must set forth sufficient evidence to support the claim. This typically means copies of the invoices or statement of account or other documents supporting the claim. If that is done, the proof of claim is said to be *prima facie* valid.[99] If

---

[99] Rule 3001(f)

insufficient support is attached to the proof of claim, a party in interest may object on that basis although usually the court will permit the claimant to amend the proof of claim to provide the support. The objection must contain evidence that the claim is not valid.[100]

4.2 Procedure

The objection to a claim is resolved by the court in a proceeding similar to regular litigation.[101]   Regular discovery is allowed, summary judgment is possible and the end result is a trial like proceeding. There is no right to a jury.

5.   Order of Distribution

As to secured creditors, the trustee is required to turn over to secured creditors their collateral if the same has not been sold or abandoned by the time the trustee files the final report. Section 725.

After that, distribution of the estate is to unsecured creditors as follows: Section 726(a)

> 1) Priority creditors pursuant to Section 507;
>
> 2) other timely filed proofs of claim;
>
> 3) tardily filed proofs of claim;
>
> 4) claims for penalties, fines, etc.;
>
> 5) interest on claims;
>
> 6) the remainder is returned to the debtor.

The funds available are used to pay the administrative expenses, i.e., the first level of priority creditors under Section 507, in full, first. If there are insufficient funds to pay the first level in full, they are paid pro-rata.   If there are any funds remaining after payment of the priority

---

[100] *In re Campbell*, 336 B.R. 430 (B.A.P. 9th Cir. 2005)(objecting party must provide *some* evidence that the claim is not allowable, other than the lack of support by the creditor on the proof of claim form);
[101] Rule 9013.

creditors, those funds go to the timely filed proofs of claim, in full, or pro-rata depending on how much money there is remaining.

6.   Priorities

Priority unsecured claims pursuant to Section 507(a) are:

1)   Administrative expenses.   In general, these are all expenses incurred by the estate after the filing of the petition, including the cost of professionals hired by the trustee and income taxes incurred by the estate; Section 503

2) Unsecured Domestic Support Obligations.[102]

3) certain claims relating to involuntary bankruptcies;

4)   wages earned within 180 days of filing and to a maximum claim of $10,000;

5) employee benefit plans (with certain limits);

6)   certain claims relating to grain storage facilities and fishermen;

7) deposits up to $1,800. For example, a person makes a down payment or layaway payment on a consumer item.

8)   most taxes. Taxes incurred or generated during the administration of the bankruptcy estate are administrative expenses and thus first level priorities.

---

[102] Section 507(a) actually lists Domestic Support Obligations as the first priority. But Section 507(a)(1)(C) provides that administrative expenses of a trustee are paid before DSO.

18. THE CHAPTER 7 DISCHARGE

1. General

The end result of a chapter 7 bankruptcy is a discharge of the debtor's debts with the statutory exceptions listed below. The discharge is, in effect, a court order requiring creditors to leave the debtor alone forever. Section 524 This is sometimes called the "fresh start." The discharge applies only to individuals and is "entered" by the court clerk automatically once the time to object to the discharge has passed. It is effective to discharge debts which existed on the date the petition was filed. Section 727(b)

2. Effect of the Discharge

The discharge "operates as an injunction against the commencement or continuation of an action ... to collect, recover, or offset any such debt. It "voids any judgment at any time obtained, to the extent that such judgment is a determination of the personal liability of the debtor ...". Section 524 It does not void or erase the debt. It only stops creditors from trying to collect the debt *from the debtor or his property*. It does not prevent the creditor from exercising any other rights they may have such as suing co-debtors or guarantors of the debt. Section 524(e) The discharge does not, of course, prevent the debtor from voluntarily paying the debt after the bankruptcy. Section 524(f)

2.1 The Community Property Discharge

When a married person files chapter 7, the estate includes all of the community property owned by the debtor and his spouse. Section 541(a)(2) For that reason, the discharge protects all community property acquired by the debtor after the bankruptcy. Section 524(a)(3) If for example, only the husband files a bankruptcy petition and receives a discharge, the wife's post-bankruptcy wages are immune from seizure to pay prepetition debts as long as they stay married.

3. Effect of the Discharge on Liens

The discharge does not usually affect the enforceability of liens; that is, after the debtor receives his discharge, he has no *in personam* liability for his car payment or house payment anymore but that will not prevent the bank from repossessing the property if he does not make the payments.[103] Section 506(d).

4. Denial of the Discharge

Some chapter 7 debtors do not receive the discharge. The bankruptcy code provides in Section 727(a) that "The court shall grant the debtor a discharge, unless ..."

1) the debtor is not an individual. This means that corporations and partnerships do not receive a discharge in Chapter 7. Section 727(a)(1) Corporations may, in some cases, receive a discharge as part of a confirmed Chapter 11 Plan of Reorganization. Section 1141(d).

2) The debtor, with intent to delay, hinder or defraud a creditor, has made a fraudulent conveyance or concealed or destroyed his property within one year of filing the petition. Section 727(a)(2)

3) The debtor has failed to keep sufficient books and records (or has destroyed his books and records).[104] Section 727(a)(3)

4) The debtor lied on his schedules or failed to cooperate with the trustee in the administration of the estate, the so-called "false oath." Section 727(a)(4)

5) The debtor failed to satisfactorily explain any loss of assets. Section 727(a)(5)

6) The debtor failed to obey a lawful order of the court. Section 727(a)(6)

7) The debtor lied, hid assets, failed to obey lawful orders, etc. in connection with the bankruptcy of another. For example,

---

[103] *Long v. Bullard*, 117 U.S. 617 (1886)(rights of a secured creditor to foreclose on its collateral survive the discharge)

[104] *In re Caneva*, 550 F.3d 755 (9th Cir. Nov 2008)(debtor's admission that he kept no books establishes a prima facie case that discharge should be denied)

the debtor hides assets of a corporation that he owns that is or was itself in bankruptcy. Section 727(a)(7)

8) The debtor has already received a discharge within the past eight years. Section 727(a)(8)

9) The debtor has received a chapter 13 discharge within the last six years unless the chapter 13 plan provided for and paid at least 70% of the debtor's debts. Section 727(a)(9

10) The debtor has waived his discharge. Section 727(a)(10)

11) The debtor failed to complete "an instructional course in personal financial management." Section 727(a)(11)

12) The debtor has been convicted of a felony "which under the circumstances, demonstrates that the filing of the case was an abuse of the provisions of this title," or violated federal securities laws, or committed any criminal act, intentional tort or willful or reckless misconduct that caused serious personal injury." Section 727(a)(12)

5. Transferring or Concealing Assets

Virtually any effort by the debtor to hide his assets before the bankruptcy will result in the loss of the discharge.[105] Section 727(a)(2) Even a transfer of an asset to a bona fide creditor before filing can result in the loss of the discharge if the transfer was made with the intent to delay, hinder or defraud creditors.

5.1 Failure to Explain Loss of Assets

This is a close cousin to the charge of transferring or concealing assets. If the debtor had assets and now does not, the debtor must be able to explain where the assets went. Section

---

[105] *In re Adeeb,* 787 F.2d 1339 (9th Cir. 1986)(when property transferred to defraud creditors is recovered before the petition date, discharge is proper); *In re Bernard,* 96 F.3d 1279 (9th Cir. 1996)(closing bank account and putting cash into safe in residence to keep cash from being seized by creditors sufficient transfer to result in denial of the discharge).

727(a)(5)   Often this arises when a debtor has completed a credit application listing assets which are not listed on the schedules. The debtor must explain where the assets went or lose the discharge. The courts are not sympathetic to the confession by the debtor that he lied on the application and never owned the asset.

5.2 Failure to Keep Adequate Records

This is also close cousin to transferring or concealing assets. The debtor cannot avoid the consequences of a failure to explain the loss of assets by asserting that he did not keep books and records. Section 727(a)(3) For most debtors, a checkbook is enough but for a business person, there must be sufficient records to permit "the debtor's financial condition or business transactions to be ascertained."

5.3 Converting Non-Exempt Assets into Exempts Assets on the Eve of Bankruptcy

The debtor is permitted to convert non-exempt assets into exempt assets before filing. Common examples are taking non-exempt cash and opening a retirement account or purchasing a home. This area contains landmines however. Debtors have lost their discharge where the court concludes that the debtor went beyond typical bankruptcy planning into fraudulent conveyances.[106]

6.   False Oath

The debtor must complete the schedules truthfully and respond truthfully to all questions and request for information from the trustee.[107] Section 727(a)(4) If he does not, his discharge will be denied. The false oath must be "material" meaning that it had some effect on the administration of the estate.[108]

---

[106] *In re Beverly*, --- F.3d ---, 2008 WL 5382453 (9th Cir. Dec 2008)(transfer made as part of a divorce settlement approved by the family law court can still be grounds for denial of the discharge)

[107] *In re Beaubouef*, 966 F.2d 174 (5th Cir. 1992)(failure to list defunct and valueless corporations on his schedules sufficient to deny discharge)

[108] *In re Wills*, 243 B.R. 58 (9th Cir. BAP 1999)(omission must affect the administration of the estate to be "material")

7.   Procedure for Denying the Discharge

The debtor's discharge is automatically granted. Creditors who wish the debtor to be denied his discharge must file a complaint in the bankruptcy court beginning an adversary proceeding.[109] The trustee and the U.S. Trustee also have standing to ask the court to deny the discharge to the debtor. Section 727(c)

After the complaint is served upon the debtor, he files an answer and litigation proceeds. A trial ultimately takes place and a judgment entered. No jury is allowed since this is an equitable action. The court is required to strictly construe the facts against the objector and liberally in favor of the debtor.

7.1 Deadline to File a Complaint

This complaint must be filed within 60 days after the date first set for the meeting of creditors under Section 341(a).[110]   If it is not filed within that time, it cannot be filed later - the discharge is entered.

7.2 Settlement of the Action

A denial of the discharge action cannot be settled by the parties without notice to all creditors and an opportunity to creditors to take over the action.

8.   Revocation of the Discharge

The discharge may be revoked within one year of the date the discharge is entered if the entry was procured by fraud which could not have been discovered within the one year time deadline. Section 727(d)

---

[109] Rule 7001
[110] Rule 4004(a)

19. NON-DISCHARGEABLE DEBTS IN CHAPTER 7

1. General

Every single debt, every single claim against the debtor, no matter who it is owed to or for what reason, is discharged upon the filing of a chapter 7 bankruptcy petition except the debts listed in Section 523(a). The discharge is not actually "entered" until the statutory period of time to object to the discharge runs. The discharge however, once entered, relates back to the petition date. Section 727(b)

2. Debts Not Discharged – Section 523(a)

Nineteen particular debts are not discharged pursuant to Section 523(a). They are as follows:

1) Certain taxes. Most taxes are not discharged but income taxes for years in which the return was due more than three years ago and which was filed at least two years before the bankruptcy and is not fraudulent are discharged. Section 523(a)(1)

2) debts incurred by false representation, false pretenses or actual fraud are not discharged. Section 523(a)(2)(A) Debts incurred by means of false financial statements are not discharged. Section 523(a)(2)(B) Purchases of "luxury goods or services" aggregating more than $500 within 90 days of filing bankruptcy or cash advances aggregating more than $750 with 70 days are presumed to be non dischargeable. Section 523(a)(2)(C)

3) debts not listed where the creditor has no actual notice in time to file a proof of claim or object to the debtor's discharge.[111] Section 523(a)(3)

4) debts incurred by fraud or defalcation while acting in a fiduciary capacity or for embezzlement or larceny. Section 523(a)(4)

---

[111] *In re Beezley,* 994 F.2d 1433 (9th Cir 1993)(debt discharged in "no asset case" even if the creditor does not receive notice unless debt non-dischargeable otherwise); *In re Nielsen,* 383 F.3d 922 (9th Cir. 2004)(confirming *Beezley*)

5) child support and spousal support, known generally as Domestic Support Obligations, defined in Section 101(14A). Section 523(a)(5)

6) willful or malicious injury to another person or her property. Section 523(a)(6)

7) fines or penalties payable to a governmental unit which is not compensation for actual pecuniary loss. Section 523(a)(7) Restitution ordered as part of a criminal procedure is not discharged.[112]

8) student loans or an "educational benefit" are not discharged unless requiring repayment would be a substantial hardship to the debtor and his dependants. Section 523(a)(8)

9) claims arising from injuries sustained by the claimant where the debtor driving an automobile while legally intoxicated. Section 523(a)(9)

10) debts not discharged in a prior case. Section 523(a)(10)

11-13) debts relating to causing a bank failure. Section 523(a)(11) to (13)

14) credit card debts incurred to pay non-dischargeable taxes. Section 523(a)(14)

15) any obligation "to a spouse, a former spouse, or child . . . incurred by the debtor in the course of a divorce or separation." Section 523(a)(15)[113]

16) Homeowners Association assessments due and payable after the case was filed where the assessment relates to a pre-filing

---

[112] *Kelly v. Robinson,* 479 U.S. 36 (1986)(restitution obligations ordered as a part of a criminal proceeding are not discharged. The opinion states, we have "a deep conviction that federal bankruptcy courts should not invalidate the results of state criminal court proceedings").

[113] This debt is dischargeable in a chapter 13 case. Section 1328(a)

period when the debtor occupied the property or rented it to someone who paid him rent. Section 523(a)(16)

17) Fees imposed on prisoners. Section 523(a)(17)

18) Loans owed to pension funds, IRAs etc. Section 523(a)(18)

19) Debts owed for violations of federal securities laws. Section 523(a)(19)

2.1 Exceptions Which Do Not Automatically Survive a Chapter 7

The exceptions to the discharge listed above *automatically* survive the chapter 7 discharge *except* those under Section 523(2)(fraud); (4)(defalcation by a fiduciary); and (6)(willful and malicious injury to person or property). Those three debts *are discharged* unless the creditor timely files a complaint seeking an order declaring the debt non-dischargeable. Section 523(c)

3.   Fraud

Section 523(a)(2) is probably the most litigated section in the bankruptcy code. Debts incurred by fraud survive the bankruptcy provided the creditor files a timely complaint and prevails at trial.[114] If judgment is entered declaring the debt to be non-dischargeable, the creditor may pursue the debtor and her husband's assets after the bankruptcy proceeding is completed. A complaint must be timely filed in the bankruptcy court or the debt is discharged no matter how fraudulent the debtor's conduct.

Section 523(a)(2) has two parts:

(A) actual fraud or false pretenses, and,

(B) false financial statements.

3.1 Credit Card Obligations

Credit card companies generate the most litigation in the non-dischargeable debts area. This is probably because some people "run up" their credit cards in anticipation of filing the petition. The credit card companies rarely complain about receiving false financial statements since they commonly require minimal financial information before issuing the credit card. The credit card company therefore must prove actual fraud. As can be imagined, this is difficult for the credit card company.

3.1.1 Proving Fraud

In order to prove fraud, the credit card company must present evidence from which the court may infer fraud since the debtor will always testify that he intended to repay the debt. The courts generally look to "badges of fraud" or a list of factors which tend to show that the debtor did or did not intend to pay the charge when incurred.[115] Among these factors, are the time between making the credit card purchase and the time of the bankruptcy, whether the purchase was a luxury item, a sudden change in the debtor's buying habits and whether or not the debtor received advice from a bankruptcy attorney before making the charge.

3.2 Traditional Bank Loans

Usually the issue in a traditional bank loan case is the accuracy of the financial statements. Here there is usually a bank loan officer to whom financial statements were given and to whom representations were made. The bank must prove that the financial statements were materially false and were reasonably relied upon by the bank officer. Section 523(a)(2)(B) If the claim is that the debtor made other false representations, other than by false

---

[115] Generally known as the *Dougherty* factors, see *In re Eshai,* 87 F.3d 1082 (9th Cir. 1996). *In re Anastas,* 94 F.3d 1280 (9th Cir. 1996)(inability to repay credit card charges not sufficient by itself to establish fraud)

financial statements, to the bank, it must show that it "justifiably relied" on the misrepresentations.[116]

4.   Defalcation by a Fiduciary, Embezzlement or Larceny

Defalcation by a fiduciary is considerably more narrow than simple breach of fiduciary duties. The existence of an express trust is required[117] and the improper taking of the assets in the trust, although the "mere" failure to account for the assets is sufficient. Section 523(a)(4)

5.   Willful and Malicious Injury to Person or Property

The complaining creditor must prove that the debtor injured her person or property willfully and intended that the harm result. Willful simply means that the debtor knew of the act. Malicious means that the debtor intended the result. This is therefore limited to intentional torts.[118] It is a difficult hurdle for the creditor. Negligence, even gross negligence, is discharged unless the debtor intended the harm to occur. Breach of contract cannot be non-dischargeable under the willful and malicious test.[119]

6.   Student Loans

Student Loans or an "educational benefit" are not discharged unless requiring repayment would be a substantial hardship to the debtor and his dependants. The courts use a three part test: (1) that the debtor cannot maintain, based on current income and expenses, a "minimal" standard of living for herself and her dependents if forced to repay the loans; (2) that additional circumstances exist indicating that this state of affairs is likely to persist for a significant portion of the repayment period of

---

[116] *Fields v. Mans*, 516 U.S. 59 (1995)(creditor must establish that it "justifiably" relied on the false representations to its detriment)

[117] *Chapman v. Forsyth & Limerick*, 43 U.S. 202 (1844)

[118] *Kahwaauhau v. Geiger*, 523 U.S. 57 (1998)(doctor's negligence discharged because there was no showing that the doctor intended the harm to occur); *Lockerby v. Sierra (In re Sierra)*, 535 F.3d 1038 (9th Cir. Aug 2008)(breach of contract, even when the debtor knows of the harm to the creditor cannot be willful and malicious injury, there must be a tort)

[119] *Lockerby v. Sierra*, 535 F.3d 1038 ((th Cir. 2008)

the student loans; and (3) that the debtor has made good faith efforts to repay the loans.[120]

6.1 Declaratory Relief

When the debtor believes that the loan should be discharged, he must file a complaint for declaratory relief in the bankruptcy court. This begins regular litigation which ends in a trial with the judge declaring whether or not repayment of the loan will be an undue hardship.

6.2 Partial Discharge

The court is entitled to enter judgment that some portion of the repayment of the student loan is undue hardship and the remainder is not. In these cases, the court typically will rule that the debtor can repay a certain amount over 20 years or 10 years and that the remainder is discharged.

7.   Procedure When a Complaint is Required

As is stated above, debts arising under Sections 523(a)(2), (4) or (6) are discharged unless the creditor timely files a complaint asking the court to declare the debt to be non-dischargeable. Section 523(c)   After the complaint is served upon the debtor, he files an answer and litigation proceeds.[121]   A non-jury trial ultimately takes place and a judgment is entered either declaring the debt to be non-dischargeable as to some certain amount or ruling for the debtor.   No jury is allowed since this is an equitable action. The court is required to strictly construe the facts against the objector and liberally in favor of the debtor.[122]

---

[120] The *"Brunner* Tests" from *Brunner v. N.Y. State Higher Educ. Servs. Corp.*, 831 F.2d 395 (2nd Cir. 1987) adopted by the 9th Cir., see *In re Nys*, 308 B.R. 436 (9th Cir. BAP 2004); *In re Carnduff*, 367 B.R. 120 (9th Cir. BAP 2009)

[121] Rule 7001 et seq

[122] *Gleason v. Thaw*, 236 U.S. 558 (1915)(exceptions to discharged should be confined to those plainly expressed)

7.1 Deadline to File Complaint

The complaint must be filed within 60 days after the date first set for the meeting of creditors under Section 341(a).[123]   If it is not filed within that time, it cannot be filed later - the discharge is entered.[124]

7.2 Preponderance of the Evidence

The creditor must prove its case by a preponderance of the evidence.[125]

8.   Effect of State Court Proceedings on the Discharge

When a creditor has received a state court judgment against a debtor prior to the filing of the petition which adjudges the debtor guilty of certain conduct with respect to a particular debt, that judgment may be used in bankruptcy court to establish all or some of the factors required prove the non-dischargeability of the debt. A judgment for the amount owed typically establishes, for example, the amount owed which may not be relitigated in bankruptcy court. The creditor will use the legal concepts of *res judicata* or *collateral estoppel* to prove up his case in the adversary proceeding pursuant to a motion for summary judgment. If the state court case was actually litigated and the issue, fraud for example, was a significant issue at trial and the state court judge made a specific finding, it is likely that the bankruptcy court will use these findings to establish non dischargeability without a trial.[126]

8.1 The Bankruptcy Court Judgment

When judgment has already been entered in a non-bankruptcy court, the judgment in the bankruptcy court will merely state that the prior judgment is not discharged.

---

[123] Rule 4004(a)

[124] *Kontrick v. Ryan*, 540 U.S. 443 (2004)(failure to timely object to the untimely filing of the complaint resulted in waiver of the deadline by the debtor)

[125] *Grogan v. Garner*, 498 U.S. 279 (1991)

[126] Id.

9.   When Creditors Lose at Trial

When a creditor files a non-dischargeability complaint and loses, the creditor may be liable for the debtor's attorneys fees if the debt was a consumer debt and the court finds that the position of the creditor was not "substantially justified." Section 523(d)

10.   Reaffirmation of Debts

A debtor may reaffirm her debt to a specific creditor after Notice and Hearing and Order of the Court. Section 524(c). The effect of reaffirmation is to resurrect the debt. It is no longer discharged. If it is not paid, the debtor may be sued for non-payment of the debt and her assets seized after bankruptcy.

20.   TAXES AND MARITAL OBLIGATIONS IN CHAPTER 7 CASES

1.   Taxes

Taxes owed to the Internal Revenue Service, the state of California, or other governmental entity are treated the same as all other debts in chapter 7 with a few exceptions. The debt may be secured, priority unsecured, or non-priority unsecured or some combination of these. The debt is likely non-dischargeable but under some circumstances is discharged along with other debts.

1.1 Secured

The government is secured if it has recorded a Notice of Lien.[127] A properly recorded notice gives the IRS a lien on all of the property of the debtor. As with all secured creditors, the government has the right to seize and sell the property to which its lien attaches even if the debt is discharged. If the property is to be retained by the debtor, the debtor must pay the government the value of the property or turn it over to the IRS.

---

[127] 26 U.S.C. 6321 for the IRS.

1.2 Unsecured

If the IRS's claim is unsecured, it may or may not be entitled to priority. Section 507(a)(8) A priority tax claim is one in which the due date of the tax return was within the three years before the bankruptcy filing or which the return was not filed at least two years before the bankruptcy.[128] Taxes assessed within 240 days before the bankruptcy filing are also entitled to priority.

1.2.1 No Exemptions

There are no exemptions when the creditor is the U.S. Treasury.

1.3 Dischargeability of Taxes

Taxes which are priority are not discharged. Section 523(a)(1) Non-priority taxes are discharged. Trust funds taxes such as payroll taxes are priority and are not discharged. Section 507(a)(8)(C)

1.4 Taxes Generated During the Chapter 7

If the trustee sells property of the estate, the estate is liable for any taxes from the sale. For example, if the trustee sells a building for $1 million and the debtor's basis is $200,000, there is a taxable gain to the estate of $800,000 which the trustee must pay from property of the estate. The debtor is not liable for this tax. Likewise, if the trustee collects accounts receivable or royalties or other income which would have been taxable on receipt to the debtor, the estate is liable for the taxes. The trustee will file a tax return[129] and pay the tax. If the trustee, does not pay the tax because there are no funds in the estate, the debtor is not liable for the tax.

---

[128] The three year period is "tolled" by previous bankruptcy cases, by offers-in-compromise, by appeals and when the debtor is out of the country. *Young v. United States*, 535 U.S 43 (2002)(the "three year rules" is tolled during the time a chapter 13 is open)

[129] Form 1041

1.5 Litigation

As with other debts, the government files a proof of claim setting forth the debtor's prepetition tax obligations. The debtor may file an objection and the court will determine the amount of tax owed. The court is authorized to "determine the amount or legality of any tax." Section 505

1.6 Automatic Stay

The government is stopped by the automatic stay as are all other creditors. There are exceptions for audits or assessing taxes. Section 362(b)(9)

2.   Alimony, Child Support and Other Marital Obligations

The 2005 amendments simplified the definition of alimony and child support. These debts are now known as Domestic Support Obligations ("DSO"). Section 101(14A)   DSO is a debt owed to a spouse or a child including a governmental unit which is "in the nature of alimony, maintenance or support." There must be a court order or some sort of marital settlement agreement.

2.1 Secured

A DSO is usually unsecured but may be secured, depending on the arrangement made by the parties or ordered by the state court. As with all secured creditors, the former spouse would have the right to seize and sell the property to which the lien attaches.

2.2 Unsecured

If the DSO is unsecured, it is a priority claim. Section 507(1) It is paid by the chapter 7 trustee after the trustee pays the other costs of administration of the estate but before all other priority claims.

2.3   The Discharge

A DSO is not discharged. The debt survives the chapter 7 case automatically. Section 523(c)   The concept of "in the nature of alimony, maintenance or support" is quite broad. For example, the debtor's obligation to pay his spouse's credit card debts or her attorney's fees or health insurance may be "in the nature of spousal support" and therefore non-dischargeable. If there is a dispute, one of the spouses should file a declaratory relief action with the bankruptcy court to allow the issue to be resolved.

2.4 Other Marital Obligations

Obligations of the debtor to his ex-spouse other than DSO are also automatically not discharged to the extent that the obligation "is incurred by the debtor in the course of a divorce or separation." Section 523(a)(15)[130]

2.5 Automatic Stay

The activities of the non-filing spouse or former spouse may or may not be stopped by the automatic stay. The stay does not stop a proceeding "for the establishment or modification" of a DSO, or for a divorce except to the extent that the divorce seeks to divide the parties' property or otherwise affect property of the bankruptcy estate. Section 362(b)(2) The spouse is also not stopped from attempting to collect a DSO from property that is not property of the estate, usually meaning postpetition wages. Section 362(b)(2)(B)

2.6 Duty of the Chapter 7 Trustee re DSO

The chapter 7 trustee is required to give notice to "the holder of" a DSO of the right of the holder to use various governmental services to collect the DSO. Section 704(a)(10) When the discharge is entered, the trustee must give notice again to the spouse and to "such State child support enforcement agency" of the discharge.

---

[130] This particular debt is discharged in a chapter 13 case.

A Summary of Bankruptcy Law

PART FOUR   CHAPTER 13[131]

---

[131] The materials in this section come largely from an article by the author and James T. King published in the California Bankruptcy Journal, "*A Chapter 13 Primer for the Non-Chapter 13 Bankruptcy Attorney*," 30 Cal. Bankr. J 41 (2009). This section is printed with permission of the California Bankruptcy Journal Corporation.

21. CHAPTER 13 OVERVIEW

1. General

In a chapter 13 bankruptcy case, there is no liquidation of assets. The debtor proposes a plan to his creditors by which he will make monthly payments of as much as he can afford over a period of typically either three or five years. Generally speaking, if the total plan payments over the life of the plan exceed the amount creditors would receive in a chapter 7 liquidation, the plan will be confirmed. The monthly plan payments are made to a trustee who, in turn, distributes the funds pro-rata to the creditors.[132] The debtor retains all of his assets and receives a discharge of debts unpaid at the end of the plan period.

The vast majority of chapter 13 cases are filed by homeowners whose mortgages are in default and who desire to save their homes from foreclosure. The debtor cures the default over a three to five year period, something which cannot be accomplished in a chapter 7. Chapter 13 cases are also filed by individuals who do not qualify for chapter 7 under the means test or who have non-dischargeable debts such as taxes or child support.

2. Qualifying for Chapter 13

A chapter 13 petition may be filed only by an *individual* with regular income. Section 109(e). He or she must complete the credit counseling before filing.[133] Section 109(h). The debtor must have less than $1,010,650 of secured debt and less than $336,900 of unsecured debt. These amounts are adjusted every three years. Section 104 The debtor may operate a business as long as the debt limitations are met. Section 1304(b).

---

[132] Chapter 13 Trustees distributed more than $5 billion to creditors in 2009. See www.usdoj.gov/ust/eo/private_trustee/library/chapter13/index.htm for annual statistics.

[133] *Mendez v. Salven (In re Mendez)*, 367 B.R. 109 (B.A.P. 9th Cir. 2009)(failure to do counseling does not relieve court of jurisdiction)

2.1 Debt Limitations

The debt limitations apply to "non-contingent and liquidated" debts. Section 109(e). An example of a contingent debt is a guarantee of another's debt or a debt of a corporation owned by the debtor for which the debtor might be liable. Liquidated is more complicated but generally means that the amount of the debt can be computed without too much difficulty.[134] Eligibility for chapter 13 is generally determined by looking at the debtor's schedules.[135]

2.1.1 Liquidated Debts

If the debtor, for example, is being sued for his involvement in an auto accident, the amount of damages and therefore the amount of the debt generally will not be known until trial. The debt is unliquidated until then and will not be included to determine eligibility for chapter 13 even if the debt is obviously very high. On the other hand, if the debtor is liable under a promissory note, the debt is liquidated at the amount of the note, even if the debtor asserts a complete defense such as statute of limitations or usury. The debt is liquidated because the amount of the debt can be easily computed.[136]

---

[134] *In re Ho*, 274 B.R. 867 (B.A.P. 9th Cir. 2002)(dispute as to liability does not necessarily render a debt unliquidated); *In re Nicholes*, 184 B.R. 82, 99-91 (B.A.P. 9th Cir. 1995)(debt which is subject to ready determination and precision in computation of the amount due is considered liquidated); *In re Slack*, 187 F.3d 1070 (9th Cir. 1999)(debt is liquidated if the amount is readily ascertainable); *In re Soderlund*, 236 B.R. 271 (B.A.P. 9th Cir. 1999)(unsecured portion of secured creditor's claim should be counted as unsecured debt for determining chapter 13 eligibility).

[135] *In re Guastella*, 341 B.R. 908 (B.A.P. 9th Cir. 2006)(tentative decision of the state court "liquidated" the debt even though not final, Bankruptcy Court properly looked beyond the schedules to determine eligibility); *In re Scovis*, 249 F.3d 975 (9th Cir. 2001)(eligibility normally determined by the debtor's originally filed schedules).

[136] *In re Slack*, 187 F.3d 1070 (9th Cir. 1999)(debt is liquidated if the amount is readily ascertainable).

2.1.2 Partially Secured Debts

If the debtor, for example, owns a home valued at $400,000 on which he owes $500,000 in mortgages, it is unclear whether the $100,000 of debt over the value of the home is to be treated as secured or unsecured *for eligibility purposes*. It appears that most judges are treating the partially secured debt as unsecured for the purposes of eligibility.

2.2 Regular Income

The chapter 13 debtor must also have regular income. Although, regular income is usually wages or income from self-employment, it may come from other sources so long as the income is sufficiently stable and regular to support the plan payments. Section 101(30). Examples of possible other sources of regular income are social security, child support, unemployment income, and contributions from a family member.

2.3 No Means Test

Unlike chapter 7, there is no means test qualification to file a chapter 13 petition. There is however a modified means test form, B22C, which must be filed but it is not used to determine qualification for chapter 13; it is used to determine the plan length, i.e. a 36 or 60 month plan, and the amount of the plan payment in some cases.

3. The Chapter 13 Trustee

The Chapter 13 Trustee is a "standing trustee," that is, a full time trustee. The trustee is an active participant in the chapter 13 process. Section 1302 They are appointed by the UST. Section 1302(a) They object to plans which do not meet the requirements of the code. They make a significant effort to insure that the debtor is paying the proper amount to his creditors under the code. They have standing to pursue avoidance actions if the debtor does not do so.[137]

---

[137] *In re* Cohen, 305 B.R. 886 (B.A.P. 9th Cir. 2004)(trustee has standing to pursue avoidance actions).

4.   Benefits of Chapter 13 Filing

Chapter 13 affords several benefits to the individual debtor over chapter 7:

a)   the debtor loses no assets whatsoever;[138]

b)   the debtor may cure arrearages owed to his secured creditors;

c)   the debtor may modify the rights of secured creditors in certain limited situations;

d)   more debts are discharged than in a chapter 7;

e)   interest and penalties stop on all unsecured debt including taxes for which no lien has yet been filed;

f)   there is slightly less stigma to the filing and certainly to the successful conclusion of the chapter 13 (or so the creditor's bar tells us);

g)   the debtor may change his mind at any time and simply dismiss the case.

5.   Chapter 13 Caveats

The chapter 13 debtor must however be aware of the following:

a)   while the case may be dismissed by the debtor at any time, it also may be converted to chapter 7 by the court before it is dismissed. A dismissal would trump the conversion if entered first but until the case is dismissed, it may be converted;[139] Section 1307

---

[138] An estate is created under Section 1306,"including property specified in Section 541." Confirmation of the plan "vests all the property of the estate in the debtor," "[e]xcept as otherwise provided in the plan or the order confirming the plan." Section 1327(b). In the Central District, the standard plan form provides that the property remains in the estate until the discharge is entered or the case is dismissed. The debtor has exclusive rights to sell property of the estate. Section 1303.

[139] *Beatty v. Traub (In re Beatty)*, 162 B.R. 853, 857-58 (B.A.P. 9th Cir. 1994)(debtor's dismissal before the order of conversion was docketed was

b) property of the estate includes all postpetition earnings of the debtor and any other assets acquired by the debtor; Section 1306

c) the debtor must make plan payments for three to five years.   If the debtor's income increases, generally the plan payments must increase (unless the original plan provided for 100% payment to all creditors);

d) the debtor must pay the Chapter 13 Trustee a fee usually based on a percentage of the plan payments for the life of the plan.[140]

e) any default recorded on the debtor's property remains until the end of the plan and discharge. If the case terminates without a discharge, the secured creditor need not record a new Notice of Default.[141]

f) the discharge is not entered until the end of the plan. If the case is dismissed for any reason, there is no discharge. In fact, if the case is dismissed, for most purposes, it is treated as though it never happened. Section 349(b).

6. Co-Debtor Automatic Stay

As with all bankruptcy petitions, the filing of a chapter 13 case results in an automatic stay requiring creditors to refrain from any further collection efforts.   Section 362(a). In a chapter 13, there is also a "co-debtor stay" which stops creditors from attempting to collect a debt "from

---

effective because debtor had an absolute right to dismiss); *but see Rossen v. Fitzgerald (In re Rossen)*, 545 F. 3d 764 (9th Cir. 2008)(debtor does not have an absolute right to dismiss "if the debtor's conduct is atypical").

[140] In the Central District this is typically 11% of the plan payments. This is significant when the debtor is proposing a 100% plan since the fee will be in addition to the payment required to pay all creditors. Also when the debtor has filed the case to cure a mortgage or secured debt arrearage, he will be paying the arrearage plus the additional fee to the trustee.

[141] Likewise, the foreclosure sale itself will be continued throughout the first year of the case and may take place immediately after the case is dismissed. California Civil Code Section 2924g(c)(1)(if postponements exceed one year, a new notice is required which would be, of course, prohibited by the automatic stay).

any individual that is liable on such debt with the debtor." Section 1301. The co-debtor stay applies only to consumer debts and may be lifted if the debt is not paid in full in the plan.

22. CHAPTER 13 PROCEDURE[142]

1. The Initial Schedules

A chapter 13 bankruptcy case is commenced by filing a petition and schedules.[143] Section 301 The petition and schedules are substantially the same as a chapter 7. They include a list of all of the debtor's assets and liabilities and a Statement of Financial Affairs. Section 521(a). In addition, the chapter 13 plan must be filed within 15 days after the case is commenced.[144] The plan must be served on every creditor. If the plan is not timely filed, the case is dismissed.[145]

2. The Chapter 13 Trustee Requirements

The Chapter 13 Trustees have a lengthy list of documents and forms which must be submitted at the outset of the case.[146] Among the documents many trustees require include a business report from the self-employed individual, the debtor's income tax returns, payroll and sales tax returns, financial statements, inventories, insurance declarations, bank statements and proof of any income received by the debtor as set forth in

---

[142] In the Central District of California there are extensive local rules covering every aspect of chapter 13 procedure. See Local Rule 3015-1.

[143] Rule 1007. The filing fee is presently $274.00.

[144] Rule 3015(b)

[145] Rule 1017(c). In the Central District of California, the case is automatically dismissed if the plan and any remaining unfiled schedules are not filed on the 15th day. Local Rule 1017-2(a).

[146] Nancy Curry, Chapter 13 Trustee is Los Angeles, commented to me about this sentence: "this sounds more imperious than I view the trustee's role – at least I hope that is what I am doing – my intent is to require that the debtor meet the requirements of the Code and the Rules – if I think that is not happening I object to the confirmation."

Schedule I.[147]   The debtor usually must complete a form called a "real property questionnaire" for her home or rental property.[148]

2.1 Meeting of Creditors

About six weeks after the case is filed, the Chapter 13 Trustee holds a meeting of creditors.[149]   Section 341(a).   The debtor is required to attend.   Section 343.   At this fairly formal meeting, the debtor is questioned first by the Chapter 13 Trustee or one of his or her staff attorneys.   The debtor may be questioned by creditors, although few creditors appear as a rule.   The questions focus primarily on the assets and liabilities of the debtor, his income and expenses, and the compliance with the rules and guidelines of the Trustee.   The testimony is recorded and is under oath.

2.2 Plan Payments and Mortgage Payments

The debtor is required to make the first payment under the plan to the trustee 30 days after the petition is filed (even though the plan has not yet been confirmed).   Some trustees require the debtor to bring the initial plan payment to the 341(a) meeting.   The debtor is also required to make his regular monthly payment to his secured creditors on time, that is, the due date pursuant to the terms of the promissory note.   Section 1326(a).   If the debtor files his chapter 13 petition on the 19th of the month and the mortgage payments are due on the 20th, he must make his regular mortgage payment to the lender the next day.[150]

2.3   Payments to Personal Property Lessors

The debtor must also make the payments due to lessors of personal property directly to the lessor for "that portion of the

---

[147] The trustee often will request copies of court orders regarding child or spousal support, automobile purchase contracts, and proof of unusual or extraordinary expenses.

[148] Each of the trustees in the Central District has an excellent website. The website of Elizabeth Rojas, for example, can be found at www.ch13wla.com.

[149] Rule 2003

[150] In the Central District, the payment must be by certified check and proof must be provided by declaration to the court.

obligation that becomes due" after the petition is filed. Section 1326(a)(1)(B) If the plan provides that the payment will be part of the monthly plan payment, the debtor may reduce "the payment to the trustee" by that amount. Typically lease payments are made directly to the lessor or "outside of the plan."

2.4 Payments to Personal Property Secured Creditors

The debtor must also make an "adequate protection" payment directly to any creditor whose claim is secured by personal property. Again, if the plan provides, or is going to provide, for payment to the trustee who will then pay the secured creditor for the life of the plan, the debtor may deduct the payment made directly from the payment made to the trustee until the plan is confirmed. Section 1326(a)(1)(C).

2.5 Proof of Insurance

The debtor must provide the lessor or secured creditor proof of insurance, of any personal property subject to a lease or a secured debt, within 60 days and "continue to do so for as long as the debtor retains possession of such property." Section 1326(a)(4).

3. The Chapter 13 Plan

The Chapter 13 Plan is filed either with the petition and schedules or within 15 days after the case is commenced.[151] It is a standard "fill in the blank" type of form. Only the debtor may propose a plan. Section 1321. Creditors do not vote on the plan as is the case in Chapter 11. A confirmation hearing is held about two months after the case is filed. Section 1324(b). The Chapter 13 Trustee or any creditor may object to confirmation of the plan on the basis that the plan does not meet the requirements of the Bankruptcy Code. Section 1324(a). If the plan complies with the code, it is confirmed. Section 1325(a)(1). If not confirmed, the case is dismissed at the confirmation hearing, converted to chapter 7, or the judge gives the debtor time to amend the plan and otherwise respond to the objections.

---

[151] Rule 3015(b)

3.1 Filing Tax Returns

The plan cannot be confirmed unless the debtor has filed all tax returns "required by Section 1308." Section 1325(a)(9). Section 1308 requires the debtor to file all tax returns for the past four years "before the (first meeting of creditors)."

4. Dismissal or Conversion of Chapter 13 Case

The court may, upon request of a party in interest, dismiss or convert a chapter 13 case for cause, Section 1307(c), before or after confirmation of the plan, for a number of different reasons including;

1) bad faith[152] or,

2) if the debtor fails to pay any "domestic support obligation" which comes due after the case is filed, Section 1307(c)(11) or,

3) if the debtor fails to file any tax return which was due within the previous four years and was unfiled, or comes due after the bankruptcy case is filed. Section 1307(e).

5. Additional Obligations for the Chapter 13 Trustees

The Chapter 13 Trustee is required to give notice to the "holder of a claim for domestic support obligation" which will give that person information regarding rights to use the services of the State child support enforcement agency. When the debtor is granted a discharge, the trustee must notify the holder of the domestic support obligation claim and the State agency and provide certain information such as the last known address of the debtor. Section 1302(d).

6. Attorney's Fees in Chapter 13 Cases

In general, the amount of fees charged by attorneys in Chapter 13 cases are subject to the scrutiny of the court. Section 329. Fees are

---

[152] *In re Eisen*, 14 F.3d 469 (9th Cir. 1994)(bad faith filing); *In re Leavitt*, 171 F.3d 1219 (9th Cir. 1999)(concealment of assets and inflation of expenses could amount to bad faith warranting dismissal of petition with prejudice).

typically a fixed amount depending on the local rules in the district.[153]   If the attorney believes that his fees should be higher than this "no-look" amount, he must ask the court for approval of the additional fees in the form of a fee application. This occurs most often when post-confirmation efforts are required such as modifications to the plan, objections to claims, and motions for relief from the automatic stay.

Most attorneys will accept less than the full allowable fee as a retainer from the client. The remainder of the fee is included in the chapter 13 plan and paid by the trustee as an administrative expense ahead of the other unsecured creditors.

23.   THE CHAPTER 13 PLAN: COMPUTING THE PLAN PAYMENT AND LENGTH OF THE PLAN

1.   Overview

Only the debtor may file a chapter 13 plan. Section 1321.   This section will discuss the amount of the plan payment, the length of the plan, the liquidation test, and feasibility. Treatment of specific types of creditors is discussed in the next section.

To be confirmed the Chapter 13 plan must:

1) pay priority creditors in full, Section 1322(a)(2) and,

2) pay secured creditors the full value of their secured claim, Section 1325(a)(5) and,

3) pay the debtor's net disposable income to the Chapter 13 Trustee for at least three years, Section 1325(b)(1)(B), and,

---

[153] In the Central District, courts will allow fees of $4,000 to attorneys in non-business cases and $4,500 in business cases without the requirement of a fee application. The debtor and the attorney must, however, execute a six-page agreement called a "RARA" – a "Rights and Responsibilities Agreement" which sets forth the amount of the fees. *Law Office of David A. Boone v. U.S. Trustee (In re Eliapo)*, 468 F.3d 592 (9th Cir. 2006)(use of no-look fees appropriate), *see also* Rule 2017(b).

4) pay unsecured creditors at least as much as they would receive in a Chapter 7 liquidation (the "liquidation test"), Section 1325(a)(4), and,

5) be proposed in good faith, Section 1325(a)(7), and,

6) provide for compensation to the Chapter 13 Trustee, typically 10% of the monthly payment.

2. Computation of Monthly Plan Payment

To be confirmed, the chapter 13 plan must provide for payment of "all" of the debtor's "projected disposable income" to be received during "the applicable commitment period." The applicable commitment period is either three years or five years. Section 1325(b)(1)(B).

The specific computation method however depends on whether the debtor is a "below-median" or "above-median" debtor. An above-median debtor is a person whose annual income for the past year is greater than the median income in the debtor's state for the debtor's household size.[154] A below-median income debtor is a person whose annual income for the past year is below the median income in the debtor's state for the debtor's household size.

2.1 Current Monthly Income "CMI"

Irrespective of whether the debtor is below or above the median, the plan payment computation begins with "current monthly income," a defined term. Current monthly income ("CMI") is defined in the Bankruptcy Code as the average of the debtor's income for the six calendar months prior to the bankruptcy filing. Section 101(10A). CMI includes receipts which are not taxable income as well as receipts from other family members "on a regular basis for household expenses."

---

[154] The median income in California, effective March 15, 2009, for a one-person household is $49,182; two person, $65,097; three person, $70,684. This data can be found at
http://www.usdoj.gov/ust/eo/bapcpa/20090315/bci_data/median_income_table.htm.

2.1.1   Establishing Gross Income

Typically, of course, the current monthly income comes from wages or self-employment. The Chapter 13 Trustee will require copies of W-2 Forms and recent pay check stubs to verify this income. When the debtor's income is from self-employment, this can be more difficult. For current monthly income, it is the actual receipts for the past six calendar months, not the net income.[155]   The effect of this is that self-employed individuals are more often "above-median" debtors, which requires a five year commitment period. It does not change disposable income, as the debtor is allowed to deduct reasonable expenses from their current monthly income. Going forward, the court and the trustee will generally allow the debtor to average his income from the last year or two of actual self-employment. The plan payment may be constant, i.e., a flat amount each month or provide for 'step up' plan payments; i.e., higher monthly plan payments in months 24-60 than in months 1-24, for example.

2.2   "Disposable Income" for Below-Median Debtors

Disposable income for a below-median debtor is "current monthly income" received "less amounts reasonably necessary to be expended" for the support of the debtor and his dependants, less payment of alimony and child support, less charitable contributions, and, if the debtor owns a business, reasonable business expenses. Section 1325(b)(2).

"Amounts reasonably necessary to be expended" is generally determined by the debtor's budget, set forth on the debtor's Schedule J filed with his initial schedules. Schedule J sets forth the debtor's actual monthly expenses including payments to secured and priority creditors, rent, food, gas, insurance, education, alimony, etc.

---

[155] *In re Weigand*, 386 B.R. 238 (B.A.P. 9th Cir. 2008).

If the debtor's remaining funds after payment of these items is $600 per month, the plan must provide for payments of $600 per month. The plan payment cannot be less unless creditors are being paid in full. Offering to pay this amount does not necessarily get the plan confirmed. The treatment of specific creditors is set forth in the next chapter.

2.3 "Disposable Income" for Above-Median Debtors

Disposable income for an above-median debtor is determined through the means test form, B22C, i.e., Section 707(b)(2)(A) and (B). Section 1325(b)(3). How this works is not clear and is still being worked out by the individual bankruptcy and appellate courts. Since the B22C uses IRS charts to determine the debtor's monthly expenses, the computation may lead to a "disposable income" amount that is not realistic; either too high or too low. The 9th Circuit has recently ruled that the Bankruptcy Code is to be followed literally and if the B22C results in a negative "disposable income," no payment to unsecured creditors is required even if the debtor has the present ability to make payments.[156] Other courts, including the 9th Circuit BAP, have generally held that the B22C computations are not set in stone and that the debtor's actual disposable income going forward is the more important factor in determining the amount of the payment.[157]

---

[156] *In re Kagenveama*, 527F.3d 990 (9th Cir. 2008). This case is not particularly meaningful in the view of most practitioners and myself. A strong argument can be made for lack of good faith when the debtor offers to pay less than he obviously can afford and the trustee may seek to modify the plan immediately thereafter anyway.

[157] *Pak v. eCast Settlement Corp. (In re Pak)*, 378 B.R. 257 (B.A.P. 9th Cir. 2007)(disposable income is the starting point for determining "projected disposable income," subject to adjustment to reflect reality going forward); *Kibbe v. Sumski (In re Kibbe)*, 361 B.R. 302 (B.A.P. 1st Cir. 2007)(projected disposable income means actual income looking forward less actual expenses using the expense tables for guidance); *In re Frederickson*, 375 B.R. 829 (B.A.P. 8th Cir. 2007)(above-median chapter 13 debtor need not propose five-year plan when means test leads to a negative number); *In re Lanning*, 380 B.R. 17 (B.A.P. 10th Cir. 2007)(above-median debtor may pay less than the means test net income by showing "special circumstances").

Again, if the above-median debtor's projected disposable income is $600 per month, the plan must provide for payments of $600 per month. The plan payment cannot be less.[158]

2.4   Determination of "Amounts Reasonably Necessary to be Expended" for the Below-Median Debtor (and, to some extent, the Above-Median Debtor)

There is no "bright-line" test as to what is or is not a reasonable expense. The Chapter 13 Trustee objects routinely to a monthly telephone expense of more than $100 for example. Expenses such as cable TV, recreation expenses, are carefully reviewed. Part of the review depends on the percentage being proposed to unsecured creditors in the plan. If the plan proposes to pay 70% or 80% of unsecured debts for example, the trustee and the court are usually less picky about the debtor's budgeted monthly expenses.

2.4.1 Pension Accounts

In general, voluntary contributions to pension accounts, i.e., I.R.A.s, and the like are allowed if historically supported. Repayment of loans received from 401(k) plans are allowed. Section 1322(f).

2.4.2 Private School Tuition

The Chapter 13 Trustee often objects to payments for private school tuition unless the cost is nominal or the payment percentage to unsecured creditors is high. An exception may be made to the extent that the school functions as child care, i.e., allowing the debtor to work.

2.4.3 Student Loans

Student loans may not be paid outside of the plan even though the debt is non-dischargeable. Section 1328(a)(2). These are non-priority unsecured debts which are paid pro-rata with other unsecured creditors. When

---

[158] Courts will allow the monthly payment to be less if the plan proposes to pay all creditors in full.

the plan is completed, there will still be a balance due to the lender along with accruing interest because the debt is non-dischargeable.[159] Section 1325(b)(2)(A)(ii)

2.4.4 Charitable Contributions

When the debtor has established a pattern of making regular charitable contributions, those contributions up to "15% of gross income" may be deducted in the net disposable income computations.[160]

2.4.5 Life Insurance Premiums

The debtor may deduct reasonable life insurance premiums.[161]

2.4.6 Care of Extended Family

The trustee will object when the debtor seeks allowance of payments being made to support extended family members.

2.4.7 Other "Luxuries"

The trustee will object (and some courts will object *sua sponte*) to perceived luxuries of the debtor such as a new vehicle, or a luxury vehicle, payment of which is reducing the return to unsecured creditors significantly. Payments to a gym or summer vacation or for big screen televisions are problematic for the debtor. These payments reduce the plan payment and are not reasonably necessary to "be expended" by the debtor and her family.

---

[159] *In re Labib-Kiyarash*, 271 B.R. 189 (B.A.P. 9th Cir. 2001)(separate classification of student loans possible if the classification meets the fairness test under §1322(b)(1)).

[160] *In re Cavanaugh*, 250 B.R. 107 (B.A.P. 9th Cir. 2000)(discussing the Religious Liberty and Charitable Donation Protection Act of 1998).

[161] *In re Smith*, 207 B.R. 888 (B.A.P. 9th Cir. 1996)(life insurance premiums may be necessary expense under chapter 13).

3. Length of the Plan or the "Commitment Period"

The length of the chapter 13 Plan depends on the "commitment period." Section 1325(b)(1)(B). If the debtor is an above-median debtor, the commitment period is five years. Section 1325(b)(4)(A). If the debtor is a below-median debtor, the commitment period is three years. Section 1325(b)(4)(B). The plan may be shorter than prescribed only if it pays all creditors in full. The plan may not exceed five years. Section 1322(d)(2).

Recently the 9th Circuit ruled that an above-median debtor who has a negative disposable income as computed by use of the means test is not required to commit to a five year plan.[162]

3.1 Plan Length for the Self-Employed Debtor

The self-employed debtor's "current monthly income" is her gross receipts for the past six months, not her net self employment income.[163] Section 101(10A) If the gross receipts in the past six months exceed the median income for the debtor's household size in her state, the commitment period is five years.

3.2 Extending the Plan Period

The court may confirm a five year plan for a below-median debtor only if it finds " cause."[164] No Plan may exceed five years. Section 1322(d)(2). If the below-median debtor requires five years to cure the default on his home, for example, the court will typically find cause and permit the plan to run five years. Reasonable cause is also common where the debtor requires additional time to pay priority creditors, for example, taxes and past due child support.

---

[162] *Kagenveama*, 527 F.3d at 999 (the "applicable commitment period" requirement is inapplicable to a plan submitted voluntarily by a debtor with no "projected disposable income").

[163] *In re Weigand*, 386 B.R. 238 (B.A.P. 9th Cir. 2008).

[164] A number of persons who reviewed this commented that "cause" was no longer required in order to extend a plan beyond 36 months. The code however provides in Section 1322(d)(2) that a below-median debtor's plan may not be longer than "3 years, unless the court, for cause, approves a longer period."

4. Liquidation Analysis

The total payments made by the debtor must be more than the creditors would receive in a chapter 7. Section 1325(a)(4). The plan cannot be confirmed unless this test is met. The total payments made over the life of the plan must exceed the value of the debtor's non-exempt assets on the date of the bankruptcy filing. For example, assume the plan payment is $600. Total payments over 36 months would therefore be $21,600. That amount must be more than the creditors would receive in a hypothetical chapter 7.

5. Feasibility

The chapter 13 plan cannot be confirmed unless it is feasible. The debtor must have sufficient income to make all of the payments required under the plan. Section 1325(a)(6). This requirement may be met by having a family member offer to contribute funds each month. The family member will be required to submit a declaration promising to make the contribution as well as proof of ability to make the contributions.

5.1 Feasibility When Claims are in Dispute

Sometimes, the feasibility of the plan cannot be determined until claims issues have been resolved. For example, the Internal Revenue Service often files a Proof of Claim estimating the amount owed when the debtor is not current on filing. Taxes, as a priority claim, must be paid in full pursuant to the Proof of Claim unless and until the court determines a lesser amount is owed. The court therefore may be unable to determine whether or not the plan is feasible until the amount of the IRS claim is resolved. In this case the court will typically continue the hearing on plan confirmation to allow claims issues to be resolved.

6. Good Faith

The court is required to find that "the action of the debtor in filing the petition was in good faith."[165] Section 1325(a)(7) The most common examples of bad faith filings are multiple filings by the debtor, filing when the motive is something other than to take advantage of the bankruptcy

---

[165] *In re Warren,* 89 B.R. 87 (9th Cir. BAP 1988)(setting forth 11 factors to consider); *In re Villanueva,* 274 B.R. 836 (9th Cir. BAP 2002).

code such as to disrupt ongoing litigation, or to adversely change the rights of only one particular creditor such as the ex-spouse.

On the other hand, plans which pay nothing to unsecured creditors are common when the debtor cannot afford to pay more than he is paying. These "zero percent" plans are not bad faith by themselves.

7. Payment of Domestic Support Obligations

The plan cannot be confirmed unless the debtor has paid "all amounts that are required to be paid under a domestic support obligation, and that first became payable (after the petition date)." Section 1325(a)(8).

24. THE CHAPTER 13 PLAN: TREATMENT OF CREDITORS

1. Overview

The plan payment, computed as set forth above, is only the first part of the analysis and is not sufficient, by itself, to result in confirmation of a plan. The plan must also provide for a given treatment to certain classes of creditors.

2. Treatment of Secured Debt in the Plan

The plan must pay a secured creditor the full amount of its *secured claim*. Section 1325(a)(5). If the debtor does not have sufficient income to pay secured creditors in full, the chapter 13 plan cannot be confirmed. Remember the claim is fully secured unless the value of the collateral is less than the amount owed. In that case, the claim is bifurcated, i.e., secured to the value of the collateral and unsecured after that. Section 506(a) Some secured claims cannot be bifurcated.

2.1 Example

For example, suppose the creditor is a credit union which has a $10,000 claim secured by equipment used by the debtor in his business which is valued at $8,000. This credit union has an $8,000 secured claim that must be paid in full with interest through the plan, and a $2,000 unsecured claim that would be treated the same as other unsecured claims.

2.2 Payment of Secured Debt Under the Plan

The debtor's plan must propose to pay secured claims in full or return the collateral to the creditor.[166]   Section 1325(a)(5). When the collateral is the debtor's residence, certain vehicles or certain other personal property, the plan typically provides that the debtor will pay the regular monthly payment directly to the creditor each month. The amount to cure defaults is included in the plan payment paid to the trustee.[167]

If the collateral is an asset other than the debtor's residence, certain vehicles or certain other personal property, the plan must pay the secured claim in monthly installments with reasonable interest, irrespective of the due date or contract interest rate.[168]   The effect of this is that the debtor may re write the original loan agreement.[169]

2.2.1 Example

Suppose the debtor owes the bank $100,000 secured by rental property valued at $150,000. The loan carries interest at 12% and is due in full in six months. The debtor may propose to pay the bank $100,000 over 60 months at 8% interest. That plan will be approved by the court if the interest rate is reasonable and the debtor has sufficient income to make the payments, i.e., the plan is feasible.

---

[166] *In re Andrews*, 49 F.3d 1404 (9th Cir 1995)(creditor who does not object to plan is deemed to have accepted it)
[167] In some districts in California, even regular monthly payments to secured creditors are paid to the chapter 13 trustee.
[168] *Till v. SCS Credit Corp.*, 541 U.S. 1 (2004)(formula rate approved); *In re Pluma*, 303 B.R. 444 (B.A.P. 9th Cir. 2003), *aff'd*, 427 F.3d 1163 (9th Cir. 2005)(approving formula method of computing interest rate).
[169] See *In re Enewally*, 368 F.3d 1165 (9th Cir. 2004)(secured portion after lien is stripped must be paid in full over the plan period).

2.3 When the Collateral is the Debtor's Residence

When the collateral is the debtor's residence, the chapter 13 plan may not modify the terms of secured debt other than to cure any existing defaults.[170] Section 1322(b)(2) The allowed secured claim cannot be rewritten, in other words, to change the interest rate or due date of the loan, if it is secured by the debtor's residence. The arrearage (or default amount) may be cured over the plan period but the promissory note must be paid in full by the due date. Obviously the lender and the debtor may agree to modify the terms but short of agreement, the plan may not change the original terms.

2.3.1 Lam Motions and Judgment Liens

In the Ninth Circuit, the debtor may "strip off," that is avoid, a completely unsecured lien on the debtor's residence.[171] This is known as a "Lam Motion." Assume the residence is worth $400,000; the first lien is $450,000 and the second lien is $100,000. The second lien is completely unsecured and the lien may be avoided.[172] Once avoided, the debt is treated as unsecured. The first lien must be paid in full on the original due date and at the original interest rate.

The debtor may also strip-off a judgment lien to the extent that it impairs the homestead exemption. Section 522(f). The stripped-off portion of the debt is then treated as unsecured debt.

---

[170] *Nobelman v. American Savings Bank*, 508 U.S. 324 (1993); *In re Lee*, 215 B.R. 22 (B.A.P. 9th Cir. 1997)(first deed of trust on real estate and appliances cannot be stripped under §1322(b)(2)).

[171] *In re Lam*, 211 B.R. 36 (B.A.P. 9th Cir. 1997)(bankruptcy debtors entitled to treat wholly unsecured deed of trust as unsecured debt and avoid the lien); *In re Zimmer*, 313 F.3d 1220 (9th Cir. 2002)(approving *Lam*)

[172] Some courts require the avoidance action to be brought as an adversary proceeding under Rule 7001 and others allow avoidance by motion.

2.4 When the Collateral is the Debtor's Automobile

2.4.1 "910 Vehicles"

As to auto loans, if, the debtor purchased a vehicle "for the personal use of the debtor" within 910 days before the bankruptcy filing, and financed the purchase with a purchase money loan, "Section 506 does not apply."[173] Section 1325(a) This apparently means that the lien may not be "stripped down," i.e., bifurcated into a secured portion and unsecured portion. The debt must be treated as fully secured.[174] The debtor may however modify the terms of the secured debt, i.e., the interest rate may be reduced and defaults cured in the plan. Section 1322(b)(2) and (3). The debtor proposes to pay the lender the amount owed over the life of the plan with reasonable interest and recomputes the monthly payment based on those parameters. This payment must be made "through the plan," that is, to the trustee each month as part of the plan payment.[175] In the alternative, the debtor may simply "assume" the loan and make the regular monthly payment directly to the auto lender.

If the debtor chooses to return the 910 vehicle, the creditor is entitled to a deficiency unsecured claim.[176]

2.4.2 Other Vehicle Loans

If the vehicle is not a "910 vehicle," the debt may be bifurcated into secured and unsecured portions[177] and

---

[173] This is the so-called "hanging paragraph" because it does not have a paragraph number.

[174] *In re Trejos*, 374 B.R. 210, 215 (B.A.P. 9th Cir. 2007)(confirming that creditor must be paid in full although interest rate and length of payment could be modified since creditor did not appeal that issue).

[175] With the trustee's fee percentage added on.

[176] *In re Rodriguez*, 375 B.R. 535 (B.A.P. 9th Cir. 2007)(creditor entitled to unsecured claim); Wright v. Santander Consumer USA, Inc. (*In re Wright*), 492 F.3d 829 (7th Cir. 2007)(creditor entitled to unsecured claim).

[177] *In Assocs. Commercial Corp. v. Rash*, 520 U.S. 953 (1997), the Supreme Court ruled that property valued under Section 506(a) must be valued at "replacement value,"

re-written in the plan, that is, the debtor is required only to pay the secured portion of the debt in full with reasonable interest for a reasonable amount of time. Section 1325(a)(5)(B)(ii). Any remaining balance is paid with the unsecured class.

2.4.3 Example

Suppose the debtor owes the finance company $20,000 secured by a "910 vehicle" valued at $12,000. The plan must pay the finance company $20,000 with reasonable interest over the life of the plan or return the vehicle.[178] If the vehicle is returned to the creditor, any deficiency is an unsecured claim, paid pro-rata with the other unsecured creditors. The interest rate on the secured portion depends on current interest rates, not the contract rate between the debtor and the finance company.

2.5 When the Collateral is Other Personal Property

If, within one year before the bankruptcy filing, the debtor incurred a purchase money debt secured by "any other thing of value," Section 506 does not apply. Section 1325(a). This again apparently means that the debt must be paid in full or the asset returned.

If the collateral was purchased more than a year before the bankruptcy, the debt may be re-written in the plan, that is, the debtor is required only to pay the secured portion of the debt in full with reasonable interest for a reasonable amount of time. Section 1325(a)(5)(B)(ii).

3. Curing Defaults on Secured Debts

The Chapter 13 plan may cure defaults on secured loans over a three or five year period. Section 1322(b)(3). Obviously this is one of the primary uses of chapter 13 cases.

---

noting "Whether replacement value is the equivalent of retail value, wholesale value, or some other value will depend on the type of debtor and the nature of the property."

[178] The payment is part of the chapter 13 plan payment made to the trustee.

3.1 Example

Suppose the debtor is four payments behind on his mortgage. A Notice of Default has been recorded and the "cure amount" including late charges, foreclosure fees and all the other charges lenders dream up is $7,200. The filing of the chapter 13 essentially makes the debtor instantaneously current. He will make the next regular mortgage payment when it is due and all subsequent monthly payments directly to the creditor. He will propose a plan to pay the cure amount to the Chapter 13 Trustee over 36 months. The plan payment still must be the debtor's net disposable income and the plan length still must be three or five years unless all creditors are paid in full in a shorter period. The trustee will pay the secured creditor the amount set forth in the plan and the default will be cured.

4. Priority Creditors

The chapter 13 plan must pay priority creditors in full over the life of the plan. Section 1322(a)(2). Priority creditors are set forth in Section 507(a) and include delinquent spousal and child support, most taxes, and administrative expenses including the debtor's attorney. If the debtor cannot establish that he has sufficient income to make these payments, the plan cannot be confirmed.

5. Other Provisions Allowed in the Plan

In addition to the above, the chapter 13 plan may provide for the assumption or rejection of executory contracts, for example office leases, return of collateral, and any other appropriate provision not inconsistent with this title." Section 1322(b).

25.   THE CHAPTER 13 PLAN: CONFIRMATION PROCEDURE

1.   Overview

A hearing to consider confirmation of the chapter 13 plan takes place typically about two months after the case is commenced. Section 1324(a). Most judges hold these confirmation cases on one particular morning or afternoon court session each month.[179]   No live testimony is received by the court at the hearing.

2.   Objections by Interested Parties

Objections to confirmation of the plan must be in writing and filed with the court in sufficient time to allow the debtor and the trustee to respond.[180] The objections must be supported by admissible evidence and must set forth specific reasons why the chapter 13 plan does not comply with the code or the rules and should therefore not be confirmed. Section 1325(a)(1).   The debtor should file a written response to the objection in time to allow the court to consider the response.

3.   Objections by the Chapter 13 Trustee

Typically the Chapter 13 Trustee advises the debtor and her counsel at the meeting of creditors, or thereafter, of any objections she has to the plan and what must be accomplished to satisfy the trustee. If the oral objections are not timely satisfied, the trustee will file a written objection with the court.

4.   The Confirmation Hearing

Typically the judge calls the matter and asks the trustee whether her objections, if any, have been resolved and whether she recommends the plan for confirmation.   The trustee will advise the court at that time whether all of the plan payments and required regular monthly payments to secured creditors have been made to date. The trustee will also advise the court whether the debtor has filed her required tax returns, paid all required domestic support obligations and generally complied with the bankruptcy code and the local rules.

---

[179] Nancy Curry, chapter 13 Trustee in Los Angeles, commented once to me that at a recent hearing, the court confirmed only 22 out of 95 plans which were heard that morning. Many were continued to allow the debtor more time to come into compliance. Many cases were dismissed because the debtor had not made the required monthly payments either to the trustee or to the secured creditors.
[180] Rule 3015(f)

4.1   Chapter 13 Trustee's Recommendation

The trustee's recommendation on confirming the plan carries a lot of weight with the court.

4.2   Objections of Other Interested Parties

Once the trustee has her say, the court will consider other objections.   Often the objections restate the objections of the trustee and have therefore already been dealt with by the court.

4.3   Consent Calendar

Some courts permit a "consent calendar" meaning if there are no objections, all payments required to be made to date have been made, and the Chapter 13 Trustee recommends confirmation in advance, the plan will be deemed confirmed without an appearance by the parties.

4.4.   Payment of Domestic Support Obligations

The plan cannot be confirmed unless the debtor has paid "all amounts that are required to be paid under a domestic support obligation, and that first became payable (after the petition date)." Section 1325(a)(8).

5.   Continuances of the Confirmation Hearing

The court is typically casual about continuances to permit the debtor to "come into compliance" with the code and the rules or to otherwise resolve issues or submit further evidence needed to resolve some particular issue.[181]   Several continuances in a case are not unusual although obviously each successive continuance requires a greater showing that the delays have not been caused by the debtor.   On the hand, continuances are almost never granted if the debtor is behind on the postpetition mortgage payments or the plan payments.

---

[181] *In re Nelson,* 343 B.R. 671 (B.A.P. 9th Cir. 2006)(the debtor should be offered the opportunity to amend plan before dismissal).

6. Confirmation or Dismissal

Eventually the court will either confirm the plan, dismiss the case or convert it to chapter 7, at the confirmation hearing.

7. *Res Judicata* Effect of Entry of the Confirmation Order

Entry of the Plan Confirmation Order has *res judicata* or *collateral estoppel* effect with respect to all issues that were resolved as part of the plan confirmation process.[182]

8. Conversion to Another Chapter

The debtor has an absolute right to convert the case at any time to a chapter 7.[183] Section 1307(a) The debtor also has an absolute right to dismiss the chapter 13 case unless it has been previously converted, for example, from a chapter 7 to a chapter 13.[184] Section 1327(a). In that case the chapter 13 may not be dismissed but must be converted back to chapter 7. In addition, the court may convert the case to chapter 7 if it has not yet been dismissed. Section 1307(c).

---

[182] *In re Espinosa*, ---- F.3d ---, 2008 WL 5158728 (9th Cir Dec. 2008)(plan which provided that student loan was discharged binding on lender who did not object to the plan reversing *In re Pardee*): *In re Summerville*, 361 B.R. 133 (B.A.P. 9th Cir. 2007)(validity of promissory note not affected by plan and post-confirmation litigation of the issue is okay); *In re Brawders*, 325 B.R. 405 (B.A.P. 9th Cir. 2005)(adequate notice to creditor is required if confirmation order is to have *res judicata* effect); *In re Pardee*, 218 B.R. 916 (B.A.P. 9th Cir. 1998), *aff'd*, 193 F.3d 1083 (9th Cir. 1999)(discussing *res judicata* effect on student loan); *see also, Knupfer v. Wolfberg (In re Wolfberg)*, 255 B.R. 879 (B.A.P. 9th Cir. 2000)(confirmed chapter 11 plan *res judicata* against debtors)
[183] *In re Croston*, 313 B.R. 447 (B.A.P. 9th Cir. 2004)(debtors had an absolute right to convert from chapter 13 to chapter 7)
[184] *In re Rossen*, 545 F.3d 76 (atypical conduct can justify denial of debtor's otherwise absolute right to dismiss chapter 13 case).

26. THE CHAPTER 13 DISCHARGE

1. Overview

The chapter 13 discharge is basically the same as the chapter 7 discharge except that it is a little more broad than the chapter 7 discharge. The discharge wipes out the debtor's liability for "all debts provided for by the plan or disallowed under Section 502" with a few exceptions. The discharge however is not "entered" or awarded to the debtor until all of the plan payments have been made to the trustee and the case is over. Section 1328(a). If the chapter 13 case is dismissed for any reason at any time, the discharge is not entered.

2. Exceptions to the Discharge

The chapter 13 discharge does not discharge the following:

1)   Secured debts which extend beyond the plan period, typically long term mortgages (Section 1328(a)(1)),

2)   Debts identified in Section 523(a)(1), i.e., most taxes; (a)(2) fraud; (a)(3) creditors who do not receive notice of the bankruptcy filing; (a)(4) defalcation by a fiduciary; (a)(5) domestic support obligations; (a)(8) student loans; and (a)(9) drunk driving. Section 1328(a)(2)

3)   a fine or restitution included as part of a criminal sentence.[185] Section 1328(a)(3)

4)   restitution or damages awarded in a civil action for willful and malicious injury to a person. Section 1328(a)(4).

A finding that a debt is non-dischargeable does not change the plan or the confirmability of the plan. The unpaid portion of the debt not discharged simply survives the case and continues to be a debt when the case is finished.

---

[185] This section was added by the 1994 amendments to undo the Supreme Court ruling in *Pennsylvania Public Welfare Debt. v. Davenport*, 495 U.S. 552 (1990).

2.1 The Super Discharge[186]

The chapter 13 discharge is sometimes referred to as the super discharge because a few debts which would not be discharged under chapter 7 are discharged under chapter 13. These are willful and malicious injury to property, 523(a)(6); fines payable to a governmental agency, (a)(7); and subsections(a)(10) through (a)(19). Marital obligations, i.e., (a)(15), which are not domestic support obligations, are discharged if not paid in full in a completed chapter 13.

2.2 Complaint Required by Creditor

As in chapter 7, debts arising from fraud, defalcation by a fiduciary, or willful and malicious injury to property, are discharged unless the creditor timely files a complaint seeking a ruling that the debt is non-dischargeable.[187]

2.3 Discharge When Plan Payments are not Complete

The court may permit a plan to end and a discharge entered even though the debtor did not complete all plan payments if the failure is due to "circumstances for the debtor should not be held accountable," and the unsecured creditors have recovered more than they would have received in a chapter 7. Section 1328(b). In this case however the discharge does not include any of the non-dischargeable debts under section 523(a). Section 1328(c).

3. Effect of Less Than Full Payment Under the Plan on Non-Dischargeable Debts

A chapter 13 plan may be confirmed even though it does not provide for full payment of non-dischargeable debts, for example, student loans. In that case, the debtor remains liable for the unpaid portion of those debts along with any accrued and unpaid interest at the end of the plan. The creditor is stopped from collecting the debt by the automatic stay

---

[186] Post-BAPCPA, this is sometimes known as the "not-so-super-discharge," as BAPCPA significantly reduced the debts discharged in a chapter 13 but not in a chapter 7.
[187] Rule 4007(d)

during the life of the case but the stays ends when the discharge is ultimately entered.[188]

4. Payment of Postpetition Domestic Support Obligations

The chapter 13 discharge may not be entered at all until the debtor "certifies" that he has made all payments "required to be paid under a judicial, or administrative order, or by statute," that became payable or "are due" up to the time of the certification including prepetition payments to the extent provided for under the plan. Section 1328(a).

5. No Discharge Permitted to Prior Filers

No discharge is granted to a person who received a discharge in a previous chapter 7 or 11 if the previous case was filed within four years before the current chapter 13 was filed or if the person received a discharge in previous chapter 13 paying less than 70% to unsecured creditors within two years before this case was filed. Section 1328(f).

6. Course on Personal Financial Management

The chapter 13 discharge will not be entered unless, "after filing the petition, he completes "an instructional course concerning personal financial management described in Section 111. . ." Section 1328(g).

7. No Discharge to Certain "Bad People"

Section 1328(h) now denies a discharge to a person "to whom Section 522(q) applies" or whom there is a pending proceeding of the "kind described in Section 522(q)." Section 522(q) identifies

    1)   debtors convicted of a felony which "demonstrates that the filing of the case was an abuse of the provisions of this title," or,

    2)   debtors owing a debt, arising from, or violating various federal securities laws, or

---

[188] *In re Foster*, 319 F.3d 495 (9th Cir. 2003)(interest on nondischargeable child support continues to accrue after a chapter 13 petition is filed and survives the discharge).

3)   a debt for "any criminal act, intentional tort, or willful or reckless misconduct that caused serious physical injury or death to another individual in the preceding five years."

27.   POST CHAPTER 13 CONFIRMATION ISSUES

1. Overview

When the court enters its Order Confirming the Chapter 13 Plan, the debtor makes his regular monthly payments to the secured creditors and the plan payment to the trustee and generally gets on with his life.

2. Modifications to the Confirmed Plan

The chapter 13 plan may be modified at any time during the case. A motion and a hearing is required and a showing of "changed circumstances."[189] Section 1329

2.1 Increases in Income

When the debtor's income increases during the life of the Plan, the debtor is required to increase the monthly payment. Section 1329.   Local rules typically require the debtor to provide copies of his tax returns each year so the trustee may determine whether to require an increase in the payment.[190]   The trustee will file a motion with the court asking the court to increase the plan payments.[191]

2.2 Decreases in Income

The debtor may petition the court for a modification of the plan decreasing the plan payment if he experiences a decrease in his income or an increase in expenses. Section 1329.   The new plan payment must be sufficient to pay the priority and secured

---

[189] *In re Than*, 215 B.R. 430 (B.A.P. 9th Cir. 1997)(section 1329 does not require changed financial circumstances, but merely changed circumstances). See also Rule 3015(g).

[190] In the Central District, see Local Bankruptcy Rule 3015-1 (eff. Jan. 2008).

[191] *In re Powers*, 202 B.R. 618 (B.A.P. 9th Cir. 1996)(trustee need not show changed circumstances in order to move for modification).

claims in full.

2.3 Request to Suspend Payments

The debtor may petition the court to suspend the monthly payment due to an unplanned event. If the suspension is granted, the shortfall must still be paid by extending the plan period (but not for more than five years) or increasing future payments.

2.4 Refinancing to Pay Down the Debt

When a chapter 13 plan which provides for payment of a sum certain to creditors over a fixed period is confirmed, there is some authority which provides that the debtor may simply borrow that much and pay off the creditors in one fell swoop although the courts are not uniform in allowing this.[192]

3. Bar Date for Filing Proofs of Claim

The bar date for filing proofs of claim is 90 days after the first date set for the first meeting of creditors.[193] A governmental unit has until 180 days after the petition is filed to file its proof of claim.[194] Creditors who do not timely file a proof of claim by this date will not receive any distributions from the trustee.[195]

3.1 Objections to Claims

Although the debtor, any creditor and/or the Chapter 13 Trustee may object to claims of creditors, it is typically the debtor who objects and most often when the plan has proposed to pay all

---

[192] *In re Sunahara*, 326 B.R. 768 (B.A.P. 9th Cir. 2005)(permitting a refinance of a residence and payment to unsecured creditors of the remaining amount owed under the plan and entry of the discharge); *In re Profit*, 283 B.R. 567 (B.A.P. 9th Cir. 2002)(a modified plan must meet some of the same requirements as an original plan, including the 60-month duration limit).

[193] Rule 3002(c). This deadline applies to secured creditors as well who are bound by the terms of the plan unless they object. This probably does not apply to residential loans or a "910 vehicle." See Section 1322(b)(1).

[194] Rule 3002(c)(1)

[195] Rule 3002(a)

creditors is full. The objection is accomplished by motion[196] which must include evidence that the claim would not be allowed under the agreement or under non-bankruptcy law.[197] Section 502(b)(1)

4. Motion to Dismiss

If the debtor gets behind on the monthly payment to the Chapter 13 Trustee, the trustee will file a motion to dismiss the case. If the motion is granted, no discharge is entered and the debtor owes the unpaid portion of her debts including all applicable interest and penalties which may have accrued during the case. Section 349 It is also likely that any foreclosure pending before the case was filed will occur quickly after the dismissal, as the foreclosure process is not required to start over.

5. Motions for Relief from the Automatic Stay

If the debtor misses a regular monthly payment to a secured creditor, the creditor may file a Motion for Relief from Stay seeking permission to proceed with its non-bankruptcy remedies to foreclose or repossess its collateral. These motions are routinely granted.

5.1 Adequate Protection

Often when the debtor is confronted with a motion for relief, he will catch up the past due payments before or at the hearing on the motion. The court typically then will give the moving creditor an "adequate protection order" ("APO") which provides that if another payment is missed, the creditor may simply submit an order with a declaration attesting to the failure to abide by the APO.

---

[196] Rule 3007(a).

[197] *In re Campbell*, 336 B.R. 430 (B.A.P. 9th Cir. 2005)(objecting party must provide *some* evidence that the claim is not allowable, other than the lack of support by the creditor on the proof of claim form); *In re Garvida*, 347 B.R. 697 (B.A.P. 9th Cir. 2006)(claimant bears the burden of proof in the claims objection process, claims objection process should not be made part of the chapter 13 plan confirmation process).

6. Post-Confirmation Borrowing

If the debtor wishes to borrow money, refinance debt or enter into any loan transaction of more than $500.00 outside of the regular course of business or for medical emergencies, the debtor must obtain court authorization to complete the transaction. A party who enters into a transaction with the debtor during the case has the risk of having the debt disallowed if the debt was not incurred in the ordinary course of business. Section 1305(c).

7. Post-Confirmation Business Operations

The debtor is free to operate his business and the trustee will not interfere with business operations. The trustee may require the debtor to submit semi-annual business reports to review the ongoing income and expenses of the business.

8. Voluntary Dismissal by the Debtor

The debtor may dismiss the case at any time by filing a form requesting dismissal provided the case has not previously been converted from another chapter. Section 1307. In that case, notice and hearing is required. The debtor may also convert the case to a chapter 7 or chapter 11 at any time. A request to convert the case to chapter 11 requires notice and a hearing. Section 1307(d).

28. CHAPTER 13 PLAN COMPREHENSIVE EXAMPLES

1.   Example One

Assume the debtor's only income is social security. Her home is worth $250,000 and she owns it free and clear. She has no other debts except a recent hospital bill of $45,000. Chapter 7 will do her no good because the chapter 7 trustee will simply take the home, sell it and pay the hospital bill. Likewise she cannot get a chapter 13 plan confirmed since she does not have sufficient income. The plan would have provide for 100% of the hospital bill since that is the amount the hospital would receive in a chapter 7, or $1,250 ($45,000 divided by 36) plus $125 in trustee fees each month and her budget will not allow this size payment. In theory at least, a chapter 13 plan could provide for a refinance or sale of the residence and payment of the proceeds to creditors but there would be a feasibility issue.

2.   Example Two

Assume the debtor is five months or $3,600 behind on his house payments. He owes $7,200 in back income taxes and has $50,000 of other unsecured debts. His only assets are his home with $25,000 equity and two vehicles, one worth $15,000 on which he owes nothing and the other a recently purchased BMW on which he owes more than it is worth. His gross income is $4,000 per month and he is therefore a below-median debtor. He would compute his plan payment by taking his current monthly income of $4,000 less his necessary monthly expenses. Let's assume the net is $400 per month. The debtor would propose a 36 month plan of $400 per month. He will pay his regular mortgage payment each month directly to the bank. The plan would provide for $100 per month to cure the $3,600 arrearage on the home and $200 per month to pay the taxes, a priority claim, (no interest is required unless the IRS has an unavoidable lien). This leaves the debtor with $100 per month for his unsecured creditors or $3,600 for the 36 months. $3,600 divided by $50,000 is 7.2%. This is sufficient if it is at least as much as the unsecured creditors would receive in a chapter 7. Our debtor here has equity in his home which is exempt and the unsecured creditors would get none of it in a chapter 7. A chapter 7 trustee would however sell the one vehicle and receive $15,000 ($2,300 would go to the debtor for the exemption). This $12,700 would go first to the taxes ($7,200) leaving $5,500 for the unsecured creditors. This is more than the debtor is proposing and therefore the plan will not be confirmed. The debtor will have to figure out how to increase the monthly payments. Note, as to the BMW, i.e., the second vehicle, the debtor will have to reaffirm the debt or return the vehicle. The trustee will likely object that the plan is not proposed in good faith since returning the vehicle, a luxury vehicle, will result by itself in increased funds available to pay creditors.

3.   Example Three

John Jones operates a small plumbing business. He has two employees. Recently one employee negligently caused a fire resulting in $200,000 in damages which his insurance does not cover. He has about $100,000 in other unsecured debt. He does not own a home. He has about $50,000 of accounts receivable and non-exempt equipment. John files chapter 13 to stave off the litigation resulting from the fire. Whether his plan will be 36 months or 60 months will depend on whether he is a below-median debtor (36 months required) or an above-median debtor (60 months required). If the total of the monthly plan payments exceeds $50,000, he meets the liquidation test since that is more than the creditors would receive in a chapter 7. If the total plan payments are $60,000 over a 60 month period, for example, the $300,000 unsecured creditors would receive is roughly 20% of the amounts owed to them.

If the insurance claim is higher than $200,000, Jones may not qualify for chapter 13 since his unsecured debt would exceed the debt limit of $336,900. If the claim amount is however disputed and cannot be easily quantified, it is unliquidated and would not count when determining whether or not Jones qualifies for chapter 13. If it is unliquidated and is later determined to be $1 million, the debtor still qualifies for chapter 13 because it was unliquidated on the petition date. In that case, the insurance claim would receive a higher share of the plan payments but, in any event, the remaining amount owed would be discharged once the plan was completed.

4.   Example Four

Cindy Smith is a teller at a bank. She is four months behind on the first trust deed on her home and six months behind on the second. Her home is worth less than the amount owed to the first. She must make the regular mortgage payments to the first and a sufficient amount to the trustee to cure the arrearage on the first over five years. The second lien can be removed by a Lam Motion. The second will thereafter be treated as an unsecured debt. If Cindy is a below-median debtor, the plan payment will be determined by taking her current monthly income ("CMI") and subtracting necessary expenses. The plan period will be three years unless she requests five in order to cure the arrearage. If she is an above-median debtor, her plan must be determined by the means test, Form B22C, and must be five years (unless you follow the result in *Kagenveama*). Since it is likely that the "net disposable income" as determined by the means test will not realistically establish her ability to pay, the courts will typically look to her CMI and deduct necessary expenses.

A Summary of Bankruptcy Law

PART 5   CHAPTER 11

A Summary of Bankruptcy Law

29. CHAPTER 11 – THE PLAYERS

1. The Debtor

The debtor is the person or entity who files the Chapter 11 Bankruptcy Petition starting the bankruptcy case.

1.1 Who may file a Chapter 11 Petition?

Any person, individual, corporation, partnership or business trust may file a Chapter 11 Petition, except a bank, insurance company or similar businesses. Section 109(d).

1.2 No Business or Insolvency is required.

The debtor is not required to have a business in order to file a Chapter 11 Petition. Nor is the debtor required to be insolvent to file although that is usually the case.

2. The Creditor's Committee

Often, although not always, the UST will organize a Committee of Unsecured Creditors in a Chapter 11 case. Section 1102(a). The committee will oversee the case on behalf of all of the unsecured creditors. The committee will often retain counsel and an accountant to assist it in performing its duties. Its duties are "consult with the debtor . . . concerning the administration of the estate"; "investigate the acts, conduct, assets . . . and financial condition of the debtor"; and "participate in the formulation of a plan." Section 1103.

3. The Debtor-in-Possession

The Debtor-in-Possession, sometimes referred to as the "DIP," is the management of the debtor or the debtor himself if the debtor is an individual. The Debtor-in-Possession functions as the trustee of the chapter 11 estate. Section 1107. The Debtor-in-Possession may be replaced by a chapter 11 Trustee on a finding of "fraud, dishonesty, incompetence, or gross mismanagement." Section 1104.

4. The Office of the United States Trustee

The Office of the United States Trustee ("UST"), a branch of the United States Department of Justice, is very active in chapter 11 cases. It oversees the administration of the bankruptcy process, appointing the creditors committee, commenting on the debtor's Plan of Reorganization and requesting conversion or dismissal of the case if that appears to be appropriate. The UST presides over the First Meeting of Creditors.

30.   CONSIDERING CHAPTER 11

1.   Overview

Conceptually, chapter 11 cases may be categorized into operating business cases, single asset cases, and individuals. An operating business case is self-explanatory; the debtor owns and operates a business. Some operating cases are designated as "small business cases" with rules designed to streamline the procedure. Section 101(51C)   A single asset case is also self-explanatory, an individual (or entity) owns a building or buildings which are facing foreclosure. Section 101(51B)   There is little significance to being a single asset case. Individual chapter 11 cases are usually either operating or single asset cases. The 2005 Amendments made a number of changes designed to make the treatment of chapter 11 cases filed by individuals similar to chapter 13 cases.

2.   Factors to Consider Before Filing Chapter 11

There are several factors to consider before making the decision to file a Chapter 11 petition:

2.1 Profitability in "Business Cases"

Typically, an operating business must be making a profit, absent unsecured debt service, from current operations to have a realistic chance of successfully reorganizing (without liquidating) in Chapter 11. The debtor cannot get farther into debt after it files the petition. Furthermore, the profits generated by operations are often used to fund the plan. A plan may be funded by new investments but that is not too realistic if the business is not generating a profit. An unprofitable company realistically will have to sell its business or simply liquidate and distribute the proceeds to the creditors. A Chapter 11 will, however, give a debtor time to sell unprofitable parts of its business thereby making it profitable.

2.2 Equity in "Asset Cases"

If the purpose for the bankruptcy filing is to save a building (or home), the debtor usually must have equity in the building or the ability to pay the secured debt in full. If the building is rental property, it must generate a positive cash flow sufficient to pay all operating expenses and encumbrances during the case to have a realistic chance at reorganizing. Property in which there is no equity can be saved over the objection of the creditors but it is rare and difficult and will probably require substantial new investment from the owners. If the property is the individual debtor's home, he must be able to pay the mortgage in full according to its original terms whether it has equity or otherwise.

2.3 Debtor's Income in an Individual Chapter 11 Case

The individual debtor's income earned after the chapter 11 petition is filed is property of the estate, similar to its treatment in a chapter 13. Section 1115 More importantly, any Plan of Reorganization proposed by the individual chapter 11 debtor must provide for payment of all of his net income to his creditors for five year period. Section 1129(a)(15)(B)

2.4 Expense of Chapter 11

A Chapter 11 is a very expensive process. Attorney's fees in a fairly simple case will probably exceed $40,000. Fees of $100,000 to $300,000 and more are common in operating cases. The U.S. Trustee's Office must be paid fees quarterly which range from $325 to $10,000 depending on the total disbursements of the debtor each quarter.

2.5 Case May Not Be Dismissed

A Chapter 11 case may not be dismissed without approval of the court.[198] Section 1112(b) Most bankruptcy judges will not approve a requested dismissal unless all of the creditors agree. A Chapter 11 case will usually be converted to Chapter 7 by the court if a Plan of Reorganization cannot be confirmed.

2.6 Ownership May Not Be Retained Over the Objection of Creditors

A Plan of Reorganization which proposes to keep current ownership in place will not be confirmed over the objection of a majority of the creditors unless all creditors are paid in full or the ownership makes a substantial new investment. This is known as the "Absolute Priority Rule." Section 1129(b) This is a big reason why most chapter 11 plans which are confirmed succeed because the debtor has reached an agreement with the creditors who then vote for the plan.

2.7 U.S. Trustee Forms and Regulations

The U.S. Trustee's Office has many rules and regulations which must be followed during the pendency of the Chapter 11. The debtor's bank accounts must be closed and new accounts opened. The new accounts and checks must indicate that the bankruptcy case is pending. A lengthy report called the Monthly Operating Report ("MOR") must be completed and filed each month. Proof of insurance must be provided. Most of the items required by the OUST must be filed within 7 days of the filing.

2.8 Disclosure, Disclosure, Disclosure

The debtor must be prepared to disclose almost anything that might be relevant to its business, operations, financial condition, and history.

3.   Benefits of Chapter 11 Filing

There are numerous benefits of a Chapter 11 filing:

---

[198] Rule 1017(a)

3.1 Pressure From Creditors will Stop Immediately

The filing of the Chapter 11 petition invokes the "automatic stay." Section 362(a). This means that all creditors must immediately cease all efforts to collect their particular debt. Any pending litigation stops. Foreclosure and seizure efforts stop. Property which has been seized but not yet sold by creditors must be returned.[199]   Property in the hands of a receiver must be returned. Sections 543   This gives the debtor time to concentrate on business operations to improve profitability and work on a Plan of Reorganization.

3.2 The Debtor Will Start Accumulating Cash

The debtor is not allowed to pay any pre-petition unsecured debts once it files its chapter 11 petition. For this reason, it should start accumulating cash reserves. In fact, failure to accumulate cash over the course of the case is usually evidence that the debtor is not making a profit and probably cannot reorganize. Of course, a lender that has a lien on cash collateral will want the excess cash turned over to it. That issue is discussed in Chapter – below.

3.3 Secured Loans May Be Modified

In general, secured creditors must be paid in full with reasonable interest for a reasonable amount of time. Section 1129(b)(2)(A). In full means the total amount owed, *or* the value of the collateral if that is less than the amount owed. The effect of this is that a high interest, short term loan may be rewritten to reasonable interest for a period of years. Secured creditors generally vigorously oppose attempts by the debtor to rewrite the loan. A loan secured solely by the debtor's home may not be adjusted or changed. Section 1123(b)(5).

3.3.1 Example

Suppose the debtor owns a building worth $1 million with $1.3 million first deed of trust. In general, the

---

[199] *United States v. Whiting Pools*, 462 U.S. 198 (1983)(IRS must return property seized prepetition)

debtor must pay the secured creditor $1 million with reasonable interest for a reasonable amount of time. The remaining $300,000 is paid with the unsecured creditors. If the property is the debtor's home, he must pay the secured creditor $1.3 million at the original interest rate and due dates.

3.4 The IRS May be Paid Over Five Years

The Bankruptcy Code provides that a Plan which proposes to pay the IRS, or any unsecured government claim, in full with interest over five years from the date of the filing of the case is reasonable. Section 1129(a)(9)(C).

3.5 Unsecured Creditors Will Generally Accept a Discount

The Bankruptcy Code provides that the unsecured creditors must receive at least as much as they would have received in a Chapter 7 liquidation. Section 1129(a)(7) In essence, the value of the business and all of its assets must be given to the creditors (before the owners). The unsecured creditors usually will accept a plan which offers more to them than they would receive in a liquidation, even if that amount is substantially less than what is owed.

3.6 Orderly Liquidation

If the debtor's financial affairs cannot be reorganized, the assets must be liquidated. An orderly liquidation by management or the owners is better than a liquidation by whichever creditor obtains permission to seize assets outside of bankruptcy (i.e., wins the "race to the courthouse"). A liquidation by management is also much better than a chapter 7 liquidation.

31. OVERVIEW OF A CHAPTER 11 PROCEEDING

1.   The Initial Filing Schedules

A Chapter 11 bankruptcy case is commenced by filing a petition and substantially the same schedules as a Chapter 7 or Chapter 13.[200] Section 301   The schedules include a list of all of the debtor's assets and liabilities and a Statement of Financial Affairs.   Section 521(a).   The schedules must be filed within 15 days after a case is commenced although extensions of this deadline are common.

1.1 Credit Counseling Required for Individuals

An *individual* must obtain credit counseling before filing the chapter 11 petition. Section 109(h)

2.   The Initial U.S. Trustee Requirements

As is stated above, the U.S. Trustee's Office has a lengthy list of documents and forms they require at the outset of the case.   Among the documents they require are the debtor's income tax returns, payroll and sales tax returns, financial statements, inventories, insurance declarations, and bank statements.   The debtor must complete a lengthy form called a "real property questionnaire" for each piece of real property in which the debtor has an interest and each real property lease.   Most of these items are due within seven days after the bankruptcy filing.

2.1 Meeting of Creditors

About six weeks after the case is filed, the debtor will have to attend a meeting of creditors, convened by the U.S. Trustee's Office.[201] Section 341(a). At this fairly formal meeting, the debtor or its management is questioned first by the staff attorney for the U.S. Trustee and then by creditors, although few creditors appear as a rule. The questions focus primarily on the assets of the debtor and the compliance with the rules and guidelines of the U. S. Trustee. The testimony is recorded and is under oath.

---

[200] Rule 1007
[201] Rule 2003

3.   Cash Collateral and Debtor-in-Possession Financing

Debtors with bank lines of credit or factoring arrangements must be concerned at the outset with cash collateral issues.

3.1 Cash Collateral

Cash collateral is cash, inventory and accounts receivable which is collateral of a creditor. Section 363(a).   A creditor who has a pre-petition lien on the debtor's inventory and/or accounts receivable, has a lien on cash collateral.   The Bankruptcy Code states that the debtor may not use the creditor's cash collateral without the approval of the court. Section 363(c)(2). Stipulations with the creditor who has a lien on cash collateral must be worked out at the very beginning of the case if not before.

3.1.1 Effect on the Chapter 11 Case

The effect of this rule on the chapter 11 case is huge.   If the debtor has $100,000 in the bank on the petition date and that cash is some creditor's collateral, the debtor may not spend the cash to pay the rent, the payroll, insurance or anything else without the court's approval in advance. It is not uncommon for a chapter 11 case to fail at the very beginning of the case when the debtor is unable to get permission to use cash collateral.

3.1.2 Rental Income

Rental income received by the debtor post-petition is the cash collateral of the bank which holds a lien on the building which is generating the rent.   This rent may not be used by the debtor without the secured creditor's permission or the court's permission.

3.2 Debtor-in-Possession Financing

As an alternative to obtaining permission to use cash collateral, some debtors will obtain "DIP Financing" before or after filing the chapter 11 case. Often the DIP financing lender is the same bank which provided prepetition credit to the debtor. The DIP financing lender will agree to lend new funds to the debtor in exchange for a postpetition lien on the debtor's assets. As cash collateral is collected during the case, the debtor uses it to pay off the prepetition loans. The debtor pays its postpetition operating expenses with the new borrowed funds. DIP financing must be approved in advance by the court.

4.   The Disclosure Statement and Plan of Reorganization

4.1 When a Plan Must Be Filed

The Plan of Reorganization is not due at any particular time. Generally it is filed four to ten months after the case is started. For the first four months of the case, only the debtor may file a plan. Section 1121(b) This is called the "exclusivity period." The exclusivity period may be extended by the court for cause. After the case is four months old, creditors may file a plan if the exclusivity period is not extended. Creditor plans are very rare.

4.2 The Disclosure Statement

The creditors vote yes or no on the proposed Plan of Reorganization. They must be given sufficient information to allow them to determine how to vote. The presentation of a Plan of Reorganization to the creditors must, therefore, be accompanied by a Disclosure Statement. Section 1125 The concept of the Disclosure Statement is similar to that of a prospectus. It contains everything a person who was going to invest money into this enterprise would reasonably want to know. The Disclosure Statement must be approved by the court as containing adequate information before it can be sent to creditors. Section 1125(a)

4.3 The Plan of Reorganization

The Plan of Reorganization divides the creditors into classes and explains how each class is to be treated once the plan is confirmed. Section 1122 It should be thought of as a new contract between the debtor and its creditors. The Plan of Reorganization will explains how the plan is to be implemented, i.e., through a sale of property, new loans, new investments or profits from business operations. Section 1123(a)(5)

5. Confirming the Plan of Reorganization

Once the Disclosure Statement has been approved by the court, it is sent to the creditors with the Plan of Reorganization and a ballot. A hearing is set for about two months later. At the hearing, the debtor announces the results of the balloting. If each class has voted for the plan, the plan is usually confirmed. If a class of creditors has voted no, the debtor can ask the court to confirm the plan anyway. Section 1129(b) This is called the "cram down" powers of the court.

6. The Final Decree

Once the Plan of Reorganization has been confirmed, the debtor takes the steps required by the plan such as making payments, selling or transferring property. Once the plan has been "substantially consummated" and no further activities are pending before the bankruptcy court, the debtor files a Motion for Final Decree.[202] Entry of the Final Decree closes the case. Section 350

7. Other Matters During the Case

7.1 Leases and Executory Contracts

The debtor must assume or reject its leases and other executory contracts during the case. The assumption or rejection may be part of the plan, however often the assumption or rejection takes place before the plan is submitted. This is because the assumption of a lease is not necessarily assured and the assumption may be critical to the success of the debtor. Section 365

7.1.1 Cure Defaults

Before the debtor may assume a lease or other executory contract, it must cure all defaults and provide adequate assurance of the ability to perform in the future. Section 365(b)

---

[202] Rule 3022 See *In re Ground Systems, Inc.*, 213 B.R. 1016 (B.A.P. 9th Cir. 1997) (setting forth factors for substantial consummation).

7.1.2 Commercial Leases

When the debtor is a tenant of non-residential real property, the lease must be assumed or rejected within 120 days after the case is filed or the lease is deemed rejected and the debtor must surrender the property. Section 365(d)(4).

7.2 Claims Issues

The amount owed by the debtor to each particular creditor must be resolved at some point during the case. In general, the amount of the debt is the amount that was owing to the creditor on the petition date and includes all amounts owed based on the agreement between the parties or pursuant to non-bankruptcy law. The amount owed generally is the amount the debtor lists in its schedules unless the listing indicates that the debt is disputed, contingent or unliquidated. In that case, or when the creditor disagrees with the amount in the debtor's schedules (or when the creditor is not listed at all), the creditor must file a Proof of Claim.[203] If the debtor or any other creditor disagrees with the basis for or the amount of the Proof of Claim, they may object. If the matter cannot be resolved at the hearing on the debtor's objection, it will be litigated in bankruptcy court much the same as any litigation outside of bankruptcy.

7.2.1 Bar Date

The debtor, at some point during the chapter 11 case, will ask the court to set a "bar date." This is the date by which creditors must file Proofs of Claim or have their claim barred. The bar date is usually a few months into the case.

7.3 Fee Applications

Professionals may not be paid during the bankruptcy case until the fees are approved by the court. A fee application may be filed only once every four months. Section 331. The fee

---

[203] Rule 3003(b)

application is a fairly big job for the professional and some judges are hesitant to allow fees during the case at all.[204]

7.4 Litigation

7.4.1 Pending Litigation

Pending pre-petition litigation against the debtor is stopped automatically once the bankruptcy petition is filed. Section 362(a) Litigation in which the debtor is the plaintiff proceeds unaffected by the automatic stay. Employment of debtor's counsel must however be approved by the bankruptcy court.

7.4.2 Postpetition Litigation

The debtor may commence litigation in bankruptcy court or in state court during the bankruptcy case. For example, the debtor may file declaratory relief actions to determine the rights of other persons in property of the estate. Creditors may also commence litigation post-petition in bankruptcy court. Examples would be actions to determine the dischargeability of a debt or the enforceability of an agreement.

7.4.3 Preference Litigation

The chapter 11 debtor should commence preference avoidance actions against creditors who have received preferences. Section 547 Typically, the debtor does not do this as the debtor is usually trying to get creditors to support the reorganization. Preference litigation often occurs after the plan is confirmed and often the right to proceed with the litigation is assigned to the creditor's committee as part of the plan.

7.5 Motions for Relief From Stay

Secured creditors will often file a Motion for Relief from Stay during the chapter 11 case. Section 362(d) This is a request

---

[204] Rule 2016

that they be allowed to ignore the bankruptcy and foreclose on their collateral. These motions are denied early in the case if there is equity in the property or the creditor is otherwise adequately protected.

7.5.1 Single Asset Cases

In a "single asset case," the debtor must file a plan within 90 days or begin monthly payments. Section 362(d)(3) If not, the court will grant relief from the stay upon application of the secured creditor. A single asset case is one in which the debtor owns a single piece of real estate, other than residential property with fewer than four units, which property generates substantially all of the gross income of the estate. Section 101(51B)

7.6 Sales of Assets

The debtor is authorized by the bankruptcy code to sell its assets "in the ordinary course of business" without court approval. Section 363(c). All other sales must be approved by the court. Section 363(b). Sales outside the ordinary course of business are typically "subject to overbids."

7.7 Tax Issues

The debtor often owes prepetition income and/or payroll taxes. The amount owed must be resolved and whether or not the debt is secured, unsecured or priority must be resolved. This is usually worked out informally with the IRS Insolvency Office. If it cannot be resolved informally, the debtor may file an objection to the IRS proof of claim or institute an adversary proceeding to resolve the issues. Section 505

7.7.1 Postpetition Tax Returns

The debtor must file all tax returns which come due after the case is filed and pay the taxes owed. Failure to do either is grounds for dismissal or conversion of the case. Section 1112((b)(4)(I)

7.8 Status Conferences

Most judges in the Central District of California set one or more Status Conferences early in the case. Section 105(d)   A Status Report is usually required to be filed prior to the hearing.

7.9 Motions to Dismiss or Convert the Case

The U.S. Trustee's Office often files a Motion to Dismiss or Convert the case during the chapter 11. Section 1112   The basis for the motion case is "cause," for which a laundry list is set forth in the code. The most common reason is the failure of the debtor to comply with all of the rules and regulations of the U.S. Trustee. The U.S. Trustee will also file a motion if the case is getting old or if the U.S. Trustee believes that a plan is not possible. Other creditors may also file this motion. The court will usually convert the case rather than dismiss it unless there are no unsecured creditors or no equity in any property of the estate.

32.   CASH COLLATERAL AND DEBTOR-IN-POSSESSION FINANCING

1.   General

The debtor is authorized to operate its business during the Chapter 11 proceeding. Section 1108   It may not, however, use cash collateral without permission of the creditor or the court. Section 363(c)(2). The effect of this rule can result in the debtor's case ending at the beginning. The court will not allow the debtor to use cash collateral and will close down the business unless the secured creditor whose lien includes cash collateral is adequately protected.

1.1 Definition of Cash Collateral

Cash collateral is cash, accounts receivable, inventory and rent, owned by the debtor, which is the collateral of some creditor. Section 363(a). It does not matter if the security interest arises pursuant to a security agreement or pursuant to law, i.e., a tax lien.

1.2 Rationale for the Rule

The bankruptcy code provides that a secured creditor's security interest does not attach to property acquired post-petition irrespective of the terms of the agreement. Section 552(a). The situation arises when a lender has a lien on all cash, accounts receivable etc "now owned or hereinafter acquired." The code provides that the "hereinafter acquired" portion of the agreement has no further effect once the bankruptcy case is filed. Therefore, when the creditor has a lien on "all cash now owned or hereinafter acquired," for example, the lien does not attach to cash acquired *after* the case has been filed. If the debtor spends the cash on hand at the beginning of the case, the secured creditor is left without its collateral. Thus the debtor may not spend the cash, for any reason, without permission of the creditor or the court. The cash must be sequestered and left untouched until court approval is obtained. Section 363(c)(4).

1.2.1 Example One

Suppose that the debtor owes $200,000 to bank on the petition date and the bank has a perfected blanket lien on all of the debtor's assets including all assets acquired until the loan is paid off. The bank's lien will not attach to any assets acquired after the petition is filed. Its lien is limited to the assets on hand on the date of filing.

1.2.2 Example Two

Suppose the debtor in example one has $100,000 of cash on the date of filing the petition. The debtor may not spend that cash without permission of the court, even if that means that the business must be closed down.

2. Adequate Protection

The court will allow the debtor to use cash collateral when the secured creditor is adequately protected. In other words, when the secured creditor is assured of getting repaid at least as much as it would have received on the petition date. Adequate protection is defined as 1) periodic payments equal to the decrease in the value of the collateral; or, 2) a replacement lien; or, 3) the indubitable equivalent. Section 361

2.1 Periodic Payments

The periodic payments must be equal to the decrease in the value of the collateral being used.[205] If the collateral is cash, inventory or accounts receivable, the periodic payment would be equal to the cash collateral used. In other words, if the debtor spends $50,000 of cash or sells $50,000 of inventory, or spends $50,000 of collected rent, that asset is gone forever; it has decreased to a value of zero. The periodic payment would have to be equal to the collateral used if the debtor was going to provide adequate protection in this manner.

2.2 Replacement Lien

This is a common form of adequate protection. The debtor gives the secured creditor a lien on assets acquired postpetition (or other assets on hand at the beginning) to replace the cash collateral used. The replacement lien given cannot exceed the amount of cash collateral used postpetition. The debtor then asks the secured creditor for permission to use x amount of cash collateral for which it will give the creditor a lien on postpetition assets equal to x.

2.3 Indubitable Equivalent

The code provides that the debtor may give the creditor the indubitable equivalent as adequate protection. Section 361(3) This is something which insures that the secured creditor's position or interest in its collateral does not erode during the pendency of the case.

3.   Obtaining Court Approval

The debtor should immediately begin negotiations with the creditor who has a lien on cash collateral. In fact, the debtor should start the negotiations before filing. Once the debtor reaches an understanding with the creditor regarding use of cash collateral, the agreement must be approved by the court.[206] The creditor will be unwilling to allow use of

---

[205] *United Savings Assn. v. Timbers of Inwood Forest,* 484 U.S. 365 (1988)(adequate protection required only when property is decreasing in value postpetition)
[206] Rule 4001(d)

cash collateral until the court has approved the agreement since it is always possible that the court will not approve the agreement between the parties and further negotiations must take place.

3.1 Shortened Notice

The bankruptcy court is required to "act promptly" on cash collateral matters. Section 363(c)(3). It will, almost always, hear a Motion for Permission to Use Cash Collateral on shortened notice. The motion should be filed at the same time as the petition. The court will probably set a hearing for the next day or two. At the hearing however, the court will usually approve the use of cash collateral for only a short period of time, to allow the business to survive until all parties in interest can be given adequate notice and an opportunity to object.

4.   Negotiation Strategies

The creditor with a lien on cash collateral has extraordinary leverage on the debtor and they know it! The creditor will immediately demand a replacement lien on all post-petition acquisitions and monthly payments. It will probably also demand a monthly or weekly budget and a series of reports during the pendency of the case. The creditor will allow the debtor to use cash collateral only pursuant to the budget by line item and only for a short period perhaps two months. They will demand that any expenditures over the budget require the creditor's advance approval. They will request extreme penalties for violation of the cash collateral stipulation, such as relief from stay without notice or automatic conversion of the case. They will demand waivers from the debtor of any actions it may have against the lender and an acknowledgment of the amount owed. The creditor often demands a "drop dead date," that is, a date by which a Plan of Reorganization must be confirmed.

4.1 Debtor's Response

The debtor should not be afraid to seek approval of the court without the creditor's acquiescence. The debtor need only to provide adequate protection. Most judges realize that the creditor is trying to strengthen its position at the outset at the expense of the other creditors. If the creditor is adequately protected, the court will allow the use of cash collateral over the creditor's objection. On the other hand, if the court disagrees that the creditor is adequately protected, it will deny the use of cash collateral and the debtor will have to immediately agree to the creditor's demands (or more of them) or find another way to finance the operations or close down.

5.   DIP Financing

Often banks will propose DIP financing instead of a cash collateral stipulation. The bank will agree to loan the debtor new funds post-petition. The arrangement will require that all cash collateral received by the debtor be paid directly, in full, to the bank until the outstanding obligation is paid in full. The bank will, in turn, lend new funds to the debtor to finance operations. The new loans will be pursuant to a budget and probably for a short period of time i.e., a few months. The new loans will be secured by all post-petition assets acquired by the debtor.

5.1 Debtor's Response

The effect of this arrangement is that the prepetition secured debt will often be paid in full before the plan is confirmed. The new debt is postpetition and is therefore an administrative expense. Administrative expenses must be paid in full on confirmation unless the creditor agrees otherwise or the plan cannot be confirmed. Section 1129(a)(9)(A) Typically the bank in this case will not demand immediate repayment but will simply continue the financing arrangement when the case is over. The debtor however must have its post-confirmation financing worked out since it has no leverage over this lender.

6.   Example One

Assume the debtor is a small retail store. On the date of filing, it has $5,000 in the bank, $50,000 of inventory and $25,000 of fixtures and equipment. Finance Company is owed $25,000 and has a lien on all cash and inventory of the debtor. The cash and inventory may not be used by the debtor postpetition without permission. A replacement lien in the post-petition cash and inventory will probably be sufficient to provide adequate protection. Finance Company will probably demand a new lien in the equipment as well. Even if the debtor were to agree to this demand, the court would probably not approve it since it substantially improves the position of one creditor and reduces the options of the debtor during the case.

7.   Example Two

Assume that the debtor is a limited partnership which owns a large apartment building. The rent acquired post-petition is the cash collateral of the mortgage company. It must be segregated until the court approves use of cash collateral. The court will usually approve, without too much trouble, the use of the rent by the debtor to pay the operating expenses of the building. The court will rarely allow the use of rent to pay compensation to the debtor's insiders or attorney's. The court will probably require the debtor to make a regular monthly payment to the bank and segregate any remaining funds. When there is insufficient funds to make a regular payment, the court will usually require the debtor to simply pay the balance each month to the bank. In this situation, the court will be concerned about the prospect of a successful reorganization and restrict the use of rent to only absolutely necessary items. If there is a junior lienholder, the senior lienholder will usually vigorously oppose the use of any funds to pay the junior, even if there are excess funds. This is because the funds are gone forever once they are spent and banks like to have as much collateral as possible.

8.   Example Three

Assume the debtor is a manufacturing company. Pre-petition it has a "factoring" arrangement with a bank in which the bank loans the debtor 60% of its accounts receivable on a day to day basis. When the receivables are collected, 100% of the funds are used to pay down the loan. The debtor pays its bills by borrowing new funds each day according to new accounts receivable generated each day. The bank has a lien on all assets of the debtor. The bank will want this arrangement approved by the court before it will continue to lend new funds because the bank cannot receive a lien on new accounts receivable, acquired by the debtor post-petition without court approval.

33. THE AUTOMATIC STAY IN CHAPTER 11 CASES

1. General

The basics of the automatic stay are set forth in Chapter 12 above. The stay is an injunction which requires all creditors to stop any efforts they were making to collect their particular debt from the debtor. Automatic stay litigation is common in chapter 11 cases.

2. Scope of the Stay

The automatic stay is fairly specific. It does not stop everything. Specifically, the automatic stay, prevents and stops any act by any entity: Section 362(a)

a) to commence or continue a judicial, administrative, or other action or proceeding against the debtor or against property of the estate:

i) that was or could have been commenced before the bankruptcy was filed; or,

ii) attempts to recover a claim that arose before the bankruptcy was filed; or,

b) to enforce a judgment, obtained before the case was filed; or,

c) to create, perfect or enforce any lien against property of the estate (or property of the debtor which is not property of the estate if the lien secures a claim that arose before the bankruptcy petition was filed); or,

d) to obtain possession or exercise control over property of the estate; or,

e) to setoff any debt owing to the debtor that arose before the case was filed against any claim against the debtor.

3.   What the Stay Does Not Stop

The stay specifically does not stop 28 different categories of activities including the following: Section 362(b)

1) criminal actions. Section 362(b)(1) This includes "quasi-criminal" governmental actions where the agency is enforcing a law for the benefit of the public;

2) family law actions. commencement or continuation of (i) the establishment of paternity; or (ii) the establishment or modification of an order for alimony, maintenance, or support; or for the collection of alimony, maintenance, or support from property which is not property of the estate except an individual debtor's postpetition earnings; Section 362(b)(2)

3) tax agency actions: (A) an audit by a governmental unit to determine tax liability; (B) the issuance to the debtor by a governmental unit of a notice of tax deficiency; (C) a demand for tax returns; Section 363(b)(9)

4) eviction actions by a landlord when the lease ends by its terms before or after the petition date; Section 362(b)(22) and (23).

4.   Relief From the Stay

A creditor may file a motion with the court asking for relief from the stay, that is, the right to proceed with its remedies notwithstanding the filing of the bankruptcy.[207] Section 362(d)   Relief from stay in chapter 11 cases is fairly rare, at least early in the case, and is limited to certain situations. The code provides that a creditor "shall" be granted relief from stay by the court:

a) for cause;

b) for lack of adequate protection;

c) when the debtor has no equity in the property and the property is not needed for an effective reorganization;

---

[207] Rule 4001

d) as to single asset cases, if the debtor does not begin making monthly payments or file a plan within 90 days.

4.1 Cause

Relief for cause is very rare and usually arises in one of two situations:

4.1.1 Bad Faith

When the debtor has filed the bankruptcy in bad faith, failed to follow the rules and regulations of the court and/or the U.S. Trustee's Office or failed to follow a previous order of the bankruptcy judge, the court will grant relief for cause. The bad faith must relate to misuse of the bankruptcy code or the system. There must have been multiple filings; new debtor syndrome i.e., forming a corporation and transferring property to it immediately prior to filing a chapter; filing bankruptcy to avoid an otherwise proper state court order; filing bankruptcy with no desire to reorganize.

4.1.2 Continue Litigation by a Creditor

Sometimes the creditor desires to continue non bankruptcy court litigation notwithstanding the bankruptcy filing. Again, this is very rare. This happens most often when the litigation involves third parties, or when the non-bankruptcy court is better equipped to resolve the litigation. It also occurs when the creditor is seeking to obtain a judgment against the debtor solely for the purpose of pursuing insurance owned by the debtor. The benefit to the creditor must outweigh the burden to the debtor, for example, where a jury is in place or even the trial is imminent, and the issue must be resolved at some point by some court, the burden to the debtor in allowing the matter to proceed is small but the benefit to the system of having the issue resolved is great. In this case, the court will allow relief to proceed to trial but not to collect on the judgment.

4.1.3 Continue Litigation by the Debtor

Sometimes when the creditor has sued the debtor prepetition, the debtor desires to proceed. For example, the debtor may have won at trial and now seeks attorneys fees. The action is stayed and the debtor must seek relief. Or the debtor may have lost at trial and wants to proceed with the appeal. The debtor must obtain relief before the matter may proceed.

4.2 Adequate Protection

This provision of the code applies only to secured creditors. Section 361 The court must grant relief unless the creditor's interest in the property is adequately protected. The concept of adequate protection is that the secured creditor's right to seize the property must not be dissipated by the delay in foreclosing during the bankruptcy proceeding. The debtor must give the secured creditor its collateral or adequate protection. Adequate protection is defined by the code as periodic payments equal to the decrease in the value of the creditor's interest in the collateral;[208] a replacement or additional lien in other property; or the "indubitable equivalent." Section 361. Sometimes the creditor is adequately protected by the "equity cushion," that is the equity in the property behind the creditor. But where there is little or no equity, the debtor must insure that the creditor does not become worse off by the delay caused by the automatic stay.

4.3 No Equity and Not Needed for an Effective Reorganization

No equity means that the total liens are greater than the value of the property. If there is no equity and the property is not needed for an effective reorganization, then any creditor who asks for relief for the purpose of pursuing its rights in that property should be granted relief. In a chapter 11, the issue of "needed for an effective reorganization" is analyzed in terms of the likelihood

---

[208] *United Savings Assn v. Timbers of Inwood Forest*, 484 U.S. 365 (1988)(adequate protection required only when the property is decreasing in value postpetition)

of the debtor confirming a Plan of Reorganization within a reasonable term.[209]

4.4 Comprehensive Example

Assume that the debtor owns the following piece of property with the following liens attached:

Building	F.M.V.	$1,000,000
1st Deed of Trust		200,000
2nd Deed of Trust		700,000
I.R.S. Tax Lien		300,000

The first deed of trust holder is adequately protected by the equity cushion behind him; $1,000,000 less $200,000 leaves $800,000 or 80%. This is especially true if the property is not decreasing in value. The second deed of trust holder has only $100,000 of equity behind him. His cushion is slim. If he can establish that the property is decreasing in value, he can demand adequate protection payments. The I.R.S. has no equity behind it. In fact, it is really only partially secured, $100,000 worth. Section 506(a) It too has the right to adequate protection only if the property is decreasing in value.

In this example, the debtor has no equity. Therefore, upon a properly noticed motion, any creditor which asks will be granted relief to foreclose if the property is not needed for an effective reorganization.

5. Modifications of the Automatic Stay

The court may modify the automatic stay in lieu of simply granting relief. It may, for example, permit a secured creditor to record a notice of default but not a notice of sale, or, permit a creditor to seize some property but not sell it.

---

[209] Id.

6.   Violations of the Automatic Stay

Acts taken in violation of the automatic stay are void.[210]   If, for example, a secured creditor files a notice of default after the petition has been filed thus violating the automatic stay, the notice of default is void. It does not have to be set aside because it is without legal effect as a matter of law.

The code provides for penalties for willful violation of the automatic stay. The code provides that any individual injured by a willful violation of the automatic stay "shall recover actual damages, including costs and attorney's fees, and, in appropriate circumstances, may recover punitive damages." Section 362(h). Unfortunately there is no redress for an unknowing violation of the automatic stay except the requirement that the unknowing violator undo or fix whatever he has done.

34.   FORMULATING THE PLAN OF REORGANIZATION

1.   General

In almost all successful Chapter 11 cases, the Plan of Reorganization is agreed to by the creditors, that is, they vote for the plan. This is, in part, because of the specificity of the cram down rules; in part, because the unsecured creditors usually will receive a greater return through a plan than through liquidation and, in part, because the fees and costs involved in litigating a cram down battle are usually prohibitive. At its most basic, the plan will be successful if it gives the creditors at least as much as they would receive in a liquidation. That is, the entire value of the assets of the debtor, including the value of the business as a going concern, must be given to the creditors according to their priorities up to 100% of the creditor claims.

2.   Negotiating With the Creditors

All negotiating with the creditors takes place within the background of the cram down rules.   Sections 1129(a) and (b)   The debtor and the

---

[210] *In re Schwartz,* 954 F.2d 569 (9th Cir. 1992)

creditors both know that the court will approve a plan which meets all of the cram down requirements. The negotiations then tend to be each party trying to get a little more than they would receive in a cram down battle.

3.   Timing

The Plan of Reorganization is not due at any particular time during the chapter 11 case. Only the debtor however may file a plan during the first 120 days of the case. Section 1121(b) This is known as the exclusivity period. The exclusivity period may be extended on a showing of good cause. The plan should be filed as soon as possible, especially if the debtor can formulate a plan that is confirmable. If a plan has not been filed within one year in most cases, the court and creditors are going to assume that a confirmable plan is not possible.

4.   Cram Down Litigation

If a class of creditors has voted against the Plan of Reorganization, the court will set a hearing to consider the debtor's request to cram down the class. This is an evidentiary hearing similar to a trial which can be enormously expensive. The issues at the hearings are likely to be values of property, reasonableness of interest rates and the debtor's ability to perform the plan. Proving values requires appraisers. Proving interest rates requires interest rate experts. Proving the debtor's ability to perform requires accountants. The parties are allowed to take the depositions of each other's experts and to cross examine them at the hearing.[211] The hearing may last for several days.   This is why successful cases usually result in plans approved by the creditors; neither party wants to spend the money to litigate the cram down (and the debtor usually cannot afford it anyway).

5.   Dividing the Creditors into Classes

The debtor must first divide its creditors into classes. A class of creditors is a group of creditors with similar rights. Only creditors with similar claims may be placed into a class. Section 1122 Secured creditors are almost always in a class by themselves since no secured creditor has the same rights as another secured creditor. Therefore, each secured creditor is a separate class. Unsecured creditors are usually all included in one class

---

[211] As this would be a "contested matter," most of the discovery rules apply. Rule 9014

together since each unsecured creditor usually has the same rights as each of the other unsecured creditors.

5.1 Example

A common breakdown of classes is as follows:

Class 1   Secured Creditor A   (If there is more than one secured creditor, it would be placed in a separate class designated as Class 1B, 1C etc. or Class 2, 3 etc).

Class 2   Unsecured Creditors. (Often, insider's claims will be placed into a separate class, perhaps Class 2B).

Class 3   Owners (or shareholders, partners etc).

5.2 Importance

The concept of classes is very important. To say that the creditors "voted for the plan" means that each *class* voted for the plan. If a class votes against the plan, that class must be crammed down according to the cramdown rules. If only one class votes against a plan, only it must be crammed down. It is common for a secured creditor, always in a class by itself, to threaten to vote against the plan to obtain more favorable terms than the debtor usually wants to give.

5.3 Voting

A class is deemed to have accepted the plan if it is unimpaired, or, if more than half of the creditors in the class that vote, vote for the plan *and* more than two-thirds of the dollars that vote, vote for the plan. Section 1126(d)

5.4 Unclassified Claims

Some creditors are not placed into classes. This is because their rights are set by the code and therefore they are not entitled to vote. The most common unclassified classes are the debtor's attorneys and other professionals, all other administrative expenses, and pre-petition, unsecured priority taxes.

6.   The Cram Down Rules

There are approximately 15 cram down rules. Section 1129(a) and (b) This will discuss the most significant seven rules.

6.1 Secured Creditors

The claim of a secured creditor is fixed as of the date of filing the bankruptcy petition, the same as all creditors. The amount owed as of the date of filing is the amount which would have been allowed had suit been filed in state court on the petition date, i.e., the amount owed under the agreement plus late charges, attorneys fees etc. This is because Section 502(b) requires the disallowance of unmatured interest, as stated above.

In the chapter 11 plan, a secured creditor must be paid the full amount of its secured claim with reasonable interest for a reasonable amount of time.[212] Section 1129(b)(2)(A)   Obviously, the secured creditor can agree to take less but the court will approve, over the secured creditor's objection, a plan which pays the creditor the full amount of its secured claim with reasonable interest for a reasonable amount of time

6.1.1 Full Amount of Secured Claim

The secured creditor's "allowed secured claim" is the amount it is owed or the value of the collateral if that value is less than the amount owed. For example, if the creditor is owed $50,000 secured by a truck worth $40,000, the creditors claim is bifurcated into an allowed secured claim of $40,000 and an allowed unsecured claim of $10,000. These claims will be placed into two separate classes and it will be entitled to vote in each class. The

---

[212] *In re Boulders on the River, Inc.,* 164 B.R. 99 (9th Cir. BAP 1994)(converting construction loan to permanent loan with 25 year amortization and 7 year balloon – 9% interest approved)

claim is secured to the extent of value in the collateral and unsecured to the extent of any excess.[213]   Section 506(a).

In the event the collateral is worth more than the creditor's claim, the creditor is "oversecured."   An oversecured creditor must be paid post petition interest, including interest at the default rate in the loan documents, and other usual costs and expenses provided by the agreement out of which the claim arose. That is, the claim of the oversecured creditor is the amount owed as of the petition date, pursuant to the agreement, plus postpetition interest, costs, fees etc. up to the value of the collateral. Section 506(b)

6.1.2 Example One

Suppose the creditor is owed $50,000 secured by a first priority lien on a truck worth $40,000. A plan which proposes to pay the creditor $40,000 with 10% interest fully amortized over three years has a decent chance of being confirmed over the creditor's objection (assuming that 10% is reasonable interest and three years is a reasonable amount of time). The remaining $10,000 is paid with the unsecured creditors' class.

6.1.3 Example Two

Suppose the creditor is owed $900,000 secured by a first deed of trust on a building worth $1 million. A plan which proposes to pay the creditor $900,000 with 8% or 9% interest, amortized over thirty years with a balloon payment due in seven years has a decent chance of being confirmed over the creditor's objection if the remainder of the cram down rules are met. Again, if the secured creditor votes no, it may present experts at the confirmation hearing establishing that the cram down

---

[213] Rule 3012 The "value of the property" is determined by the court if the parties cannot agree on the value. A party will file a motion to determine value under Section 506(a). This should, obviously, be completed before the plan is filed.

rules, most significantly the interest rate, stretch-out period and feasibility, have not been met.

6.1.4 Example Three

Let us assume the collateral is real property worth $500,000 of the date of filing the petition. The first trust deed holder is owed $350,000 on the date of filing; the second, $125,000 and the third, $100,000. The first will be entitled to postpetition interest, costs and attorneys fees because it is oversecured. The second will be entitled to postpetition interest, costs and fees until the value of the claims of the first and second equal $500,000, because until then, they are both oversecured. After that, the secured claim of the second will go down to the extent the claim of the first keeps going up since both claims cannot be more than $500,000. The claim of the third is fixed as of the date of filing since it is not oversecured. The secured claim of the third is $25,000 and the unsecured claim is $75,000. No post petition interest will be allowed on either portion. In fact, the third may immediately seek relief from stay on the basis that there is no equity in the property for the debtor.

6.1.5 Unreasonable Discrimination

It is common that the debtor will have more than one secured creditor. It is also common that one secured creditor will make harsher demands than another. In general, the debtor is not allowed to "unreasonably" discriminate amongst the creditors. Section 1129(b)(1)

6.1.6 Leaving the Creditor "Unimpaired"

If the debtor is current on some particular secured obligation or can bring the loan current before or at confirmation, the debtor can propose in the plan that the debtor will simply pay the creditor according to the original terms of the loan agreement. This is known as leaving the creditor unimpaired. An unimpaired creditor does not get to vote on the plan. It is deemed to have accepted the plan. Section 1126(f) If the debtor changes any term of the loan, no matter how small or insignificant, the creditor is impaired and may vote on the plan. This causes practical problems at times. The debtor may wish to leave a secured creditor unimpaired for two reasons: 1) the interest rate in the original loan is lower than current reasonable interest or 2) the creditor is particularly hostile and the debtor wants to defuse the hostility. If the debtor however is going to pay some secured creditor a higher than reasonable interest rate (to, in effect "buy" its vote), other creditors may claim that the debtor is unreasonably discriminating in favor of one particular class.

6.1.7   Curing the Secured Creditor Making it "Unimpaired"

Again, the debtor may cure a secured debt as part of the plan, that is pay the amount in default bringing the loan current. This is done when the loan terms are better than "reasonable interest for a reasonable amount of time." It is also done when the oversecured secured creditor is demanding default interest post-petition. When the plan cures the loan, the creditor has the right only to the contract interest from the petition date.[214]

6.2 Unsecured Creditors

Unsecured creditors must be paid at least as much as they would receive in a chapter 7 liquidation. Section 1129(a)(7)(A)(ii) The plan cannot be confirmed unless this requirement is met, in other words, it cannot be waived unless literally every creditor votes for the plan. This, obviously, requires a valuation of all of the assets of the debtor, including the value as a going concern.

---

[214] *In re Entz-White Lumber and Supply Co.*, 850 F.2d 1338 (9th Cir. 1988), see also *In re Future Media Productions, Inc.*, 547 F.3d 956 (9th Cir. Oct 2008)(cure must be part of the plan, cure before the plan does not relate back to the petition date and therefore the creditor has the right to default interest)

6.2.1 Liquidation Analysis

The debtor must prepare a complete liquidation analysis and include it in the Disclosure Statement. It must include the value of each asset and an appraisal if the issue of value of some particular asset is important. The analysis must show the creditors how much they would receive in a liquidation compared to how much they will receive under the plan.

6.2.1.1 Valuation

Valuation analysis depends largely on the proposed use of the property by the debtor. If the debtor is returning the property, the valuation would be the "fire sale" price. If the debtor is retaining the property, it is a "going concern" value which is obviously higher than liquidation.

6.2.2 Example One

Suppose the unsecured creditors are owed $500,000. A plan which proposes to pay the creditors $200,000 over three years (for example) will be confirmed if $200,000 is more than the class would receive in a chapter 7 liquidation. The remainder of the cram down rules must be met, most importantly the absolute priority rule (see below).

6.3 Taxes

Taxes which are secured or priority must be paid in full with reasonable interest over a period of not more than five years from the date of the petition. Section 1129(a)(9)(C). The IRS will usually not oppose a plan to pay it over five years unless they believe that the debtor simply cannot make the payments. If the taxes are neither secured nor priority, Section 507(a)(8), the IRS is a general unsecured creditor and will be placed in that class and paid with the other unsecured creditors.

6.4 Absolute Priority Rule

6.4.1 The Rule

This cram down rule is the downfall of most debtor plans, at the conceptual level at least. The absolute priority rule provides that no class may receive *anything* under the plan or *even retain its ownership interest* unless all senior classes are paid in full.[215] Section 1129(b)(2)(B)(ii) This is another way of saying that all of the value of the debtor's assets must go to the creditors unless the creditors support the plan.

6.4.1.1 Absolute Priority Rule in Individual Cases

The absolute priority rule does not apply to chapter 11 cases filed by individuals.

6.4.2 Effect of the Rule

The effect of this rule is that the debtor usually offers the unsecured creditors enough to coax them into voting for the plan. The rule is only relevant when there is a class of unsecured creditors who vote against the plan since secured creditors must be paid the full amount of their secured claim anyway.

6.4.3 Example

Suppose the plan offers to pay the unsecured creditors 80% of their claims and the owners retain their ownership interest. The plan will not be confirmed if the unsecured class votes against the plan because the owners are retaining their interests. If the unsecured class votes for the plan but a secured class votes against it, the absolute priority rule does not apply since the secured creditor is being paid in full.

---

[215] *Case v. Los Angeles Lumber Products Co.*, 308 U.S. 106 (1939)(plan which permits present owners to retain their interests when creditors are not being paid in full is not fair and equitable to creditors)

6.4.4 New Value Exception (i.e., There is Still Hope)

If the debtor's plan violates the absolute priority rule because the debtor is retaining its ownership interest, and a junior class of creditors has rejected the plan, the debtor's ownership can offer to pay an amount equal to the value of the interest that is being retained. In effect, the ownership is buying the remainder interest in the assets. The cost of establishing the value of the remainder interest can be significant.

6.4.4.1 Example

If the debtor is planning on paying the unsecured creditors 50% for example, and retaining ownership, the debtor will have to pay into the plan, i.e., contribute new capital, an amount equal to the value of the ownership interest that he is retaining.

6.4.4.2 Auction Required

The Supreme Court has ruled that an auction is required when the debtor proposes that it will provide new value and thereby retain its interest in the debtor.[216]

6.5 Feasibility

6.5.1 General

The court must be convinced that the debtor can perform what it promises in the plan. Section 1129(a)(11). This is, as can be imagined, a major battleground when the creditors oppose the plan. If the plan payments are going to come from profits, the debtor will have to establish that it can generate profits in the future for the life of the plan. Since the debtor was probably losing money when the case

---

[216] *Bank of America National Trust & Savings v. 203 No. LaSalle Street Partnership*, 526 U.S. 434 (1999)

was filed or had a negative cash-flow, there is a tendency not to believe the debtor's projections. If the debtor is going to borrow the money or sell something to fund the plan, the court will want the loan in place or the sale assured in order to find feasibility.

6.6 One Class Must Vote for the Plan

Congress has decided that the debtor may not cram down everyone. Therefore, at least one non-insider class who is impaired under the plan must vote for the plan. Section 1129(a)(10) Impaired means their rights are being changed under the plan. This may not seem difficult at first glance, however, all unsecured creditors will probably be in one class. The remaining classes will be secured creditors. The practical effect, then, is that one secured creditor whose rights are being changed under the plan or the unsecured class must vote for the plan.

6.7 Good Faith

This rule is very important and is often ignored by the debtor. The plan must be proposed in good faith. Section 1129(a)(3). Good faith is not defined in the code and is not easy to understand. It involves a sense by the court that the debtor is trying to maximize the return to the creditors within the confines of the rules. The sense by the court that the debtor is keeping all of his "toys," putting the risk of financial loss on the creditors, and giving them the bare minimum required in return will, in all likelihood, result in a ruling against the plan in a close case.

7. Individual Cases

When the debtor is an individual, the plan must pay the debtor's net income for a five year period unless creditors are being paid in full in less than five years. Section 1129(a)(15)(B)

35.   THE DISCLOSURE STATEMENT

1.   General

The creditors vote yes or no on a plan, whether proposed by the debtor, the creditor's committee or some other entity. In order to make a meaningful decision, they be given sufficient information. This is accomplished through the Disclosure Statement. The code states that acceptance or rejection of a plan may not be sought until "there is transmitted (to the creditors) a written disclosure statement approved, after notice and a hearing, by the court as containing adequate information." Section 1125(b).

2.   Procedure

The proponent of the plan, usually the debtor, will prepare the Disclosure Statement with the Plan of Reorganization attached thereto as Exhibit A. The Disclosure Statement is served only on the U.S. Trustee's Office, the Creditor's Committee and any person who has requested special notice.[217]   A hearing is set with a least 36 days notice to the interested parties. The purpose of the hearing is to permit the court to make a finding that the Disclosure Statement contains adequate information.

2.1 Form of the Disclosure Statement

The Central District of California has a standard form which is required by most, but not all, of the judges.

3.   Adequate Information

The code defines adequate information as "information of a kind, and in sufficient detail, as far as is reasonably practicable in light of the nature and history of the debtor and the condition of the debtor's books and records, that would enable a hypothetical reasonable investor typical of holders of claims or interests of the relevant class to make an informed judgment about the plan..." Section 1125(a).

---

[217] Rule 3017(a)

3.1 Role of the Court

The court will read and comment on the adequacy of the Disclosure Statement even if no party in interest has objected.

3.2 U.S. Trustee Comments

The U.S. Trustee's Office usually files comments or objections to the adequacy of the Disclosure Statement.

4. Strategy

Creditors who wish to defeat the debtor's proposed plan will usually vigorously oppose the requested approval of the Disclosure Statement. They will complain that the Disclosure Statement should not be approved because it does not contain adequate information and because the plan attached cannot be confirmed on its face. Secured creditors especially will attack the Disclosure Statement if they are unhappy with their particular treatment under the plan. They will want to avoid the cost of a cram down battle.

4.1 Amended Disclosure Statements

Often, in the face of objections to the adequacy of the Disclosure Statement, the debtor will amend the Disclosure Statement prior to the first hearing.

5. Required Information

The following is the minimum information required in the Disclosure Statement (taken from the "Guide to Preparation of Disclosure Statements" prepared by the U.S. Trustee's Office, May, 1994):

a) Information regarding the purpose of the Disclosure Statement.

b) Description of the debtor, its business, the reasons for the financial difficulties, and efforts to correct the problems.

c) Description of management, salaries, affiliations, and qualifications.

d) Description of the plan, the classes, amounts, and treatment of each class.

e) Disclosure of Insider Claims and circumstances giving rise to the claims.

f) Means of performing the Plan, including disclosure of source of any new funds, sale of property, continued business operations.

g) Historical and current financial information including cash flow statements, balance sheets, P & L and estimate of current values of assets.

h) Financial projections on cash and accrual basis, disclosure of assumptions used in formulating the projections, disclosure of identity of persons preparing the projections.

i) Marketing efforts to sell property, if relevant, identity of listing agents, pending offers.

j) Cash requirements on confirmation of the Plan i.e., how much cash does the debtor need to pay the claims required to be paid on confirmation. These include professional fees, administrative expenses and any initial payments to creditors. The source of the funds must be disclosed.

k) Liquidation analysis including an estimate of the amount each class will receive on liquidation of the assets of the debtor.

l) Discussion of the absolute priority rule and whether it prevents cramdown of any particular class.

m) Description of any pending or anticipated litigation.

n) Analysis of tax consequences of confirmation of the Plan.

o) Vote required for approval of the Plan.

p) Discussion of post-petition events which might affect the case.

6.   Small Business Cases

Small Business debtor's Plan of Reorganization and any creditor plans must be filed within 300 days. Section 1121(e). The Disclosure Statement may be "conditionally" approved, subject to allowing creditors to object to the adequacy of the Disclosure Statement at the confirmation hearing. Section 1125(f).

36.   CONFIRMING THE PLAN

1.   General

Once the Disclosure Statement has been approved, that is, found by the court to contain adequate information to allow the creditors to decide how to vote, it is sent along with the plan and a ballot to all persons and entities who are entitled to vote on the plan.

2.   Events Prior To Confirmation Hearing

When the court approves the Disclosure Statement, it will set a confirmation hearing and instruct debtor's counsel (or the plan proponent if other than the debtor) to give notice of the hearing to all creditors and parties in interest and to give notice of various dates and deadlines. The notice will instruct creditors to send ballots to debtor's counsel by a date certain, usually about 30 days later.[218] It will set a date by which creditors must file any objection to confirmation of the plan. That date is usually about 20 days before the hearing. It will set a date for the debtor to file either a Motion to Confirm Plan or a Plan Confirmation Memorandum. There is little difference between a Motion to Confirm Plan and a Plan Confirmation Memorandum. Which is used is simply the preference of the particular judge. If any party in interest files an objection to the plan, the debtor is given a date by which to respond.

2.1 Evidence

There must be submitted with the Motion to Confirm Plan sufficient evidence to allow the court to make a finding that all of

---

[218] Rule3017(c)

the requirements of Section 1129(a) and, if cramdown is required, Section 1129(b), have been met. The evidence is produced in the form of declarations of management, debtor's counsel and any required experts.

3. Voting Analysis

The debtor (or plan proponent) will tabulate the ballots and file a summary with the court. A class is deemed to have accepted the plan if more than half of the creditors who vote, vote for the plan and more than two-thirds of the dollars that vote, vote for the plan. Section 1126(c)

3.1 Estimation of Claims

Sometimes litigation of the nature and amount of some claims is lengthy and the procedure threatens the Plan of Reorganization process. The court must know the total amount of claims to determine whether or not a particular class voted for the Plan or not. If the litigation is going to take months or longer, the reorganization process might have to wait putting the debtor in jeopardy. This happens is cases of mass torts, for example, asbestos cases and the Dalkon shield. It also happens when the debtor is denying liability entirely and determination of the amount of damages is complex. An example might be malpractice claims against a professional or construction damages against a builder. The debtor will file a motion asking the court to estimate the amount of the claims solely for purposes of voting on the Plan.[219] Section 502(c)

4. When All Classes Have Voted For the Plan

When all classes have voted for the plan, there is usually little to do at the confirmation hearing. The court is still required to make two important findings as follows:

1) The plan is feasible; and,

---

[219] *In re Aquaslide "N' Dive Corp.*, 85 B.R. 545 (9th Cir.BAP 1987)(court has the right and duty to estimate tort claims for the purpose of confirming a plan under Chapter 11)

2) Creditors will receive more under the plan than they would receive in a liquidation (unless literally every creditor votes for the plan);

The court must make a number of other findings, such as the plan was proposed in good faith and future management is identified, however issues with respect to those matters do not come up to often.

The debtor must therefore offer evidence at the confirmation hearing that the plan is feasible and that the creditors will receive more than they would receive in a liquidation. The reality, however, is that if no person has objected to confirmation, the court will usually not delve too deeply into the issues of feasibility and liquidation analysis.

5.   When a Class Has Voted Against the Plan

When a class votes against the plan, the debtor's job is much tougher and perhaps impossible.

5.1 A Secured Class

If a secured creditor class has voted no, the debtor must offer proof that the plan pays the secured creditor 100% of its *secured* claim with reasonable interest for a reasonable amount of time and that the payments are feasible. Section 1129(b)(2)(A). This requires an appraisal of the property, an expert on interest rates and stretch out periods for this type of property, and an accountant to establish cash flow. Creditors may take the deposition of the experts, similar to any other litigation. The complaining creditor will offer its own experts to establish that the debtor has not met its burden. If there is more than one secured class, the creditor may complain that the other class was treated more favorable than it and therefore the plan unreasonably discriminates against it. Section 1129(b)(1).

The hearing can take place over several days and may be broken into parts, in other words, the value of the property may be established first and the interest rates later.

5.2 Unsecured Class

If the unsecured class votes no, the difficulty for the debtor is enormous. The biggest problems will be the new value exception to the absolute priority rule, the liquidation analysis and feasibility. Remember, if the unsecured class is getting paid in full, it is unimpaired and is not entitled to vote. Section 1126(f). Therefore, if the unsecured class is voting at all, it must be receiving less than payment in full and if the ownership is retaining its interest, the absolute priority rule is violated and the plan fails. The plan proponent may offer to put in new value equal to the value of the interest it is retaining. An expert will have to testify about the value of the interest which ownership is retaining.

6.   When Confirmation is Denied

If the court rules against the plan proponent and denies the request to confirm the plan, the chapter 11 case is not over although it is probably pretty close to over. The plan proponent may propose another plan which will likely require the submission of another Disclosure Statement for approval.   Denial of confirmation is usually pretty good grounds for conversion of the case to chapter 7. Section 1112   The U.S. Trustee will likely file a Motion to Dismiss or Convert the case shortly after the denial unless it believes that a confirmable plan is likely within a short period of time.

7.   Effect of Confirmation

The confirmation of the plan does not end the case. It does however vest all of the property of the estate into the Reorganized Debtor except as otherwise provided for in the plan. Section 1141(b)   The court retains jurisdiction to perform certain functions after the plan is confirmed. These functions are generally 1) approve final fee applications of the professionals of the case; 2) complete any pending adversary proceedings; 3) complete claims objections process, and 4) resolve any remaining issues of the case.

37.   THE CHAPTER 11 DISCHARGE

1.   General

The end result of a bankruptcy proceeding is usually a discharge of any debts not paid during the proceeding or as part of a plan. In chapter 7, only an individual receives a discharge, i.e., corporations do not receive a discharge. Corporations may receive a discharge in a chapter 11.

2.   The Chapter 11 Discharge

Confirmation of a Plan of Reorganization results in entry of a discharge of all debts of the debtor, except those provided for in the plan. Section 1141(d). This is irrespective of whether the debtor is an individual or a corporation or other entity.

2.1 No Discharge Until Entry of the Final Decree

Many courts will not "enter" the discharge until the Final Decree is entered. Typically, the Final Decree is entered when the debtor has "substantially consummated the plan," and there are no matters remaining before the bankruptcy court.

2.2 No Discharge if the Plan is a Liquidation Plan

If the Plan liquidates the corporate debtor, the debtor will not receive a discharge. Section 1141(d)(3)

3.   The Discharge in Individual Cases

The discharge is not entered in an individual case until the plan is completed. Section 1141(d)(5)

4.   What the Discharge does not Discharge

The discharge does not discharge any debts of an individual debtor which would not be discharged under Section 523(a). The discharge is denied entirely if it would have been denied under Section 727 in a chapter 7 case. Section 1141(d)(3)(C)

38.   SALES OF PROPERTY OF THE ESTATE

1.   General

The debtor is authorized to sell property of the estate in the "ordinary course of business" without court approval. Section 363(b). All other sales of property of the estate must be approved in advance by the court. The code does not define "ordinary course of business." If there is any doubt, the debtor should get permission from the court.

2.   Selling Assets Before Confirmation of the Plan

The debtor may, of course, sell some or all of its assets as part of the Plan of Reorganization. Section 1123(b)(4) The Disclosure Statement will provide all of the information needed to allow creditors and parties in interest to determine whether the sale is in the best interests of the estate. If the debtor desires to sell some specific asset before submission of a plan, the court must find a good business purpose for the sale. The court will look to the value of the asset to be sold compared to the value of all the assets of the debtor. If the value is small compared to all of the assets, the court is likely to approve the sale.[220] If the assets are a significant portion of the estate, the court will want a good reason why the sale must take place before a Disclosure Statement has been filed.

3.1 *Sub Rosa* Plan of Reorganization

Sometimes the sale of the assets is the plan. It is obvious that the only asset that will exist after the sale is cash and the "plan" will propose simply to distribute the cash to creditors according to their priorities.   The information provided to creditors and parties in interest in the sale motion is significantly less than what is required in the Disclosure Statement, and the time to object and do discovery to support the objection is streamlined to sometimes only a week or two. The debtor will argue that the sale must take place immediately or the debtor will fail and no one

---

[220] *In re Lionel,* 722 F.2d 1063 (2d Cir. 1983),

will get anything. The creditors will argue that this is really a *sub rosa* plan, i.e., the sale is a disguised plan.[221]

3. Sales Procedures

A sale of assets outside of the ordinary course of business must be approved by the court. Typically the debtor will propose to pay secured creditors, as well as the costs of sale including any broker fees, out of the sale proceeds. A motion is filed and set for hearing about 30 days later. The court must make a finding at the hearing that the sale is in the best interest of the estate, that there is a "sound business purpose for the sale,"[222] and, of course, that it is for a fair price. For this reason, these sales are usually subject to overbids. Rather than getting into a disagreement about value, the court will be satisfied if there has been extensive notice to potential buyers who are permitted to come to court and overbid.

3.1 Overbid Procedures

Often the debtor will ask the court to approve overbid procedures in advance so that potential buyers will be sure that they can actually overbid at the hearing. Procedures include how much the initial overbid will be, when the new buyer must close, how much the deposit must be and what proof the buyer must provide to establish that he can actually close if he is the highest bidder.

3.2 Break Up Fees

Often an interested buyer will ask the debtor to pay it a breakup fee in the event that it is overbid at the sale hearing. If there are several interested buyers, it can be difficult to get a buyer to pay the costs of negotiating the sale terms and agreement. The breakup fee, sometimes called a "stalking horse fee," is designed to reimburse the person who negotiated the initial agreement but was

---

[221] *PBGC v. Braniff Airways, Inc (In re Braniff Airways, Inc.)*, 700 F.2d 935 (5th Cir. 1982)(the debtor should not be able to short circuit the plan procedures set forth in the code) Unfortunately this is a common occurrence in my opinion. *In re Chrysler*, --- B.R. ----, 2009 WL 1490990 (Bkrtcy S.D.N.Y.May 26, 2009) and *In re Chrysler*, --- B.R. ----, 2009 WL 1507547 (Bkrtcy S.D.N.Y.2009)(approving sale over *sub rosa* objection)

[222] *Walter v. Sunwest Bank (In re Walter)*, 83 B.R. 14, 19 (9th Cir. BAP 1988)

outbid at the hearing. Some courts are reluctant to allow break up fees at all.[223] The fee, in any event, cannot be more than the reasonable cost of negotiating the transaction.

4.   Sales Free and Clear of Liens

The bankruptcy code permits sale of property by the debtor "free and clear of all liens." Section 363(f) This procedure is used when there is a dispute over the amount of a lien or whether the lien attaches at all.

Issues over liens are common in chapter 11 cases. Whether a lien is avoidable because it is a preference, a fraudulent conveyance, or was not properly perfected is obviously very important in determining who gets what as part of the plan or if the debtor can even reorganize. The creditor's committee may attack liens of insiders trying to expand the assets to be distributed to unsecured creditors.

4.1 Procedures

The court is authorized to approve a sale free and clear of liens, i.e., irrespective of these issues and over the objection of the lienholder only pursuant to Section 363(f). The debtor must establish that the proceeds of the sale are sufficient to pay all secured creditors in full; or, the lien is in bona fide dispute,[224] or the property could be sold free and clear of liens under non-bankruptcy law. Typically the sale order will provide the liens attach to the proceeds of the sale in whatever order they attached to the property being sold and in whatever condition.

5. Sale Orders

When the bankruptcy court approves the sale motion, it will be asked to make numerous findings designed to protect the buyer. These findings include that the sale price is fair, that the buyer is not assuming any debts or obligations of the debtor beyond those set forth in the agreement, and that, if the requirements are met, the sale is free and clear of liens, claims, encumbrances, charges etc. This "comfort order" is often

---

[223] Bruce A. Markell, *The Case Against Breakup Fees in Bankruptcy*, 66 AM. BANKR. L.J. 349 (1992)
[224] *In re Vortex Fishing Systems, Inc.*, 277 F.3d 1057 (9th Cir. 2002)(setting forth factors for determining whether a *bona fide* dispute exists)

significant to the buyer and sometimes chapter 11 cases are filed for the sole purpose of selling the assets and getting the buyer this additional protection from the debtor's other claimants.

5.1 No Appeals

A sale order cannot be appealed if the court finds that the sale was in good faith and the unhappy objecting creditor does not get a stay pending appeal. Section 363(m)

6. Forcing the Debtor to Sell an Asset

Sometimes creditors or the creditor's committee will want the debtor to sell some particular asset it does not want to sell or some buyer will want to buy an asset that the debtor does not want to sell. There is no procedure to force the debtor to sell an asset short of filing a plan which proposes to sell the asset or convincing the court to appoint a chapter 11 trustee.

39. CLAIMS LITIGATION

1. General

Debt is defined as "...liability on a claim." Section 101(12). Creditor is defined as an "...entity that has a claim against the debtor..." Section 101(10)(A). The concept of claim is considerably more broad than the concept of debt. The term claim is defined in the code as a "... right to payment, whether or not such right is reduced to judgment, liquidated, unliquidated, fixed, contingent, matured, unmatured, disputed, undisputed, legal, equitable, secured or unsecured..." Section 101(5)(A). This is very important in bankruptcy because only claims are discharged, only claims are paid as part of the liquidation or reorganization, and only the collection of pre petition claims are stopped by the automatic stay. Whatever was owed or might have been owed by the debtor on the date of filing of the petition is a claim.

2. Filing a Proof of Claim

A claim is "allowed" or "disallowed" as to some particular amount. Allowed means that the claimant will vote on the plan and will share in the distribution of the estate. Disallowed means the claimant gets nothing. In a chapter 11, if the claim is listed on the debtor's schedules and is not identified as "contingent", "disputed" or "unliquidated," no additional filing is required, it is automatically allowed in full in the amount stated in the schedules.[225] All other creditors, i.e., claimants, must file a form called a "Proof of Claim."

2.1 Who May File a Proof of Claim?

A proof of claim may be filed by the claimant, by the debtor, by the trustee or by a co-obligor of the debtor. Section 501

2.2 Due Date

In a chapter 11, the court fixes the time within which proofs of claim must be filed, usually upon application of the debtor or the trustee if there is one.[226] The due date is usually three to six months after the case is filed. It certainly does not hurt to file a proof of claim immediately.

2.3 Attachments to the Proof of Claim

The claimant must attach documents and other evidence to his Proof of Claim sufficient to make a prima facie case that the amount set forth in the Proof of Claim is the amount that is owed.[227]

3.   Objections to Claims

A claim is automatically "allowed" unless someone objects. There are eight grounds on which a party may object. Section 502(b):

1) The claim is unenforceable either under state or federal law or under the terms of the agreement under which the claim is based.

2) The claim is for unmatured interest.

---

[225] Rule 3003(b)
[226] Rule 3003(c)(3)
[227] Rule 3001

3) The claim is for property taxes which exceed the value of the property.

4) The claim is for the services of an insider or an attorney to the extent the claim is unreasonable.

5) The claim is for a debt that is unmatured and will not be discharged under Section 523.

6) If the claim is that of a lessor, it cannot exceed the greater of one years rent or 15% of the lease, not to exceed three years rent.

7) If the claim is from an employee "for damages resulting from the termination of an employment contract," it cannot exceed one years compensation.[228]

8) Relates to employment taxes.

4. Procedure

The objection to a claim is resolved by the court in a proceeding similar to regular litigation. Regular discovery is allowed, summary judgment is possible and the end result is a trial like proceeding.

4.1 Burden of Proof

The objection to the Proof of Claim must set forth evidence which disputes the basis for and/or the amount of the claim. At that point, the burden shifts back to the claimant to establish the amount owed.

4.2 Jury

There is no right to a jury in the claims objection process. Indeed a person who files a proof of claim basically waives his right to a jury in the entire bankruptcy process. In other words, any

---

[228] *In re Networks Electronic Corp.*, 195 B.R. 92 (9th Cir. BAP 1996)(Section 507(b)(7)] operates as a statutory cap to limit employment-related claims based on the future compensation an employee would have earned had the contract not been terminated); *In re Condor Systems, Inc.*, 296 B.R. 5 (9th Cir. BAP 2003)

proceeding against a claimant will necessarily involve the amount of the claim to which the claimant has no right a jury.

40. INDIVIDUAL CHAPTER 11 CASES

1. General

Individuals may file a chapter 11 petition. There is no requirement that they be insolvent or operate a business. Section 109(d). The individual must complete the credit counseling prior to filing the petition. Section 109(h)

2. Small Business or Single Asset Case

An individual chapter 11 case may also be designated a "single asset case" or a "small business case."

3. Differences Between Corporate and Individual Chapter 11 Cases

In BAPCPA, Congress attempted to make chapter 11 procedures for the individual substantially the same as chapter 13.

3.1 Property of the Estate

Property of the estate in the individual chapter 11 case is generally the same as chapter 7 but also includes all property acquired postpetition including wages earned postpetition until the case is closed, dismissed or converted. Section 1115 The debtor however remains in possession of the property.

3.2 Additional Requirements to Confirm an Individual Plan of Reorganization

3.2.1 Postpetition Earnings

The individual's chapter 11 plan must include "all or such portion of earnings from personal services performed by the debtor after commencement of the case or other future income of the debtor as is necessary for the execution of the plan." Section 1123(a)(8)   A plan proposed by someone other than the debtor may not provide for the sale of exempt property. Section 1123(c)

The court cannot confirm a plan unless the creditors are paid in full or the plan pays "not less than the projected disposable income of the debtor (as defined in section 1325(b)(2)) to be received during the five year period beginning on the date the first payment is due under the plan." Section 1129(a)(15)

3.2.2 Domestic Support Obligations

The court cannot confirm a plan unless the debtor has paid all domestic support obligations which have become due after the petition was filed.   Section 1129(a)(14)

3.3 The Absolute Priority Rule

The plan may be confirmed even though it violates the absolute priority rule. In other words, the debtor may retain his property even though the plan does not pay creditors in full. Section 1129(b)(2)(B)(ii)

3.4 The Chapter 11 Discharge

Confirmation of the plan does not result in a discharge of debts "until the court orders a discharge on completion of all payments under the plan." Section 1141(d)(5) The debtor may seek a discharge before completing the plan as long as the payments actually made exceed the amount that creditors would receive in a chapter 7 and modification of the plan is not "practicable." Section 1141(d)(5)

3.5 Modification of the Plan of Reorganization

The individual's chapter 11 plan may be modified even after the plan is substantially consummated. Section 1127(e)

4.   Saving the Individual's Home

The individual chapter 11 case is typically filed when the individual does not qualify for chapter 13 and wants to save her home. The plan must pay the home mortgage in full. Section 1123(b)(5) It cannot be bifurcated into secured and unsecured portions. A completely unsecured junior lien may be stripped in the chapter 11 as in the chapter 13.[229]

4.1 Cross-Collateralized Liens on Homes

The inability of the individual debtor to modify a loan on his home is limited to loans where the home is the only collateral. Where the creditor has additional assets as collateral, for example, inventory or other business personal property, the loan may be modified.

5.   Grounds for Dismissal of the Individual Chapter 11 Case

The individual chapter 11 case "shall" be dismissed or converted for cause including failure of the debtor to pay domestic support obligations which come due after the case is filed. Section 1112(b)(4)(P) Cause also includes failure to pay taxes "owed after" the case is filed or to file tax returns which come due after the case is filed. Section 1112(b)(4)(I)

41.   SMALL BUSINESS CHAPTER 11 CASES

1.   General

Small Business cases are defined as "a person engaged in commercial or business activities" other than operating real estate with aggregate "noncontingent liquidated secured and unsecured debts" owed to non-insiders of less than $2 million "for a case in which the United States Trustee has not appointed [a committee]" or where the court has determined that the committee has not been sufficiently active. Section 101(51B)

---

[229] *In re Lam*, 211 B.R. 36 (B.A.P. 9th Cir. 1997)(bankruptcy debtors entitled to treat wholly unsecured deed of trust as unsecured debt and avoid the lien); *In re* Zimmer, 313 F.3d 1220 (9th Cir. 2002)(approving *Lam*)

2.   Designating the Case as a Small Business Case

The small business debtor must "state in the petition whether or not the debtor is a small business debtor."[230]   This fixes the status of the case until someone objects and the court finds otherwise. If a creditor's committee is appointed, the case will not be treated as a small business case unless the court finds that the committee has not been sufficiently active to provide "effective oversight of the debtor."[231]

3.   Differences Between Small Business Cases and Other Chapter 11 Business Cases

3.1 Reporting Requirements

The small business debtor must file "periodic financial and other reports" with specified information.[232] Section 308

3.2 The Automatic Stay

The automatic stay does not apply to a small business debtor if the small business debtor "is a debtor in a small business case pending at the time the petition is filed," or filed a case that was dismissed "for any reason" in the two years before the petition date, or had a plan confirmed in the previous two years. Section 362(n)   If the debtor is an entity "that has acquired substantially all of the assets" of a small business debtor which filed a previous case, there is no stay. This "does not apply" if the debtor can prove that the filing "resulted from circumstances beyond the control of the debtor" and can get a plan confirmed.

3.3 Creditor's Committee

The small business debtor may ask the court to "order that a committee not be appointed." Section 1102(a)(4)

---

[230] Rule 1020(a)

[231] Rule 1020(c)

[232] Rule 2015(a)(6). The reports required by Section 308 must be filed monthly with the UST. This requirement, added by BAPCPA, is a little strange since all debtors are required to file "financial and other reports."

3.4 Duties of the Small Business Debtor

The small business debtor is required to file "not later than 7 days" after the petition is filed, "its most recent balance sheet, statement of operations, cash-flow statement and Federal income tax return" or a statement that none exists. Section 1116 The bankruptcy code also instructs the debtor to attend the meeting of creditors, "timely file all schedules and statement of affairs," and other requirements typical of any chapter 11 debtor. The code requires the small business debtor to "timely file tax returns" and pay all taxes which are administrative expenses.

3.5 Deadlines for the Plan of Reorganization

The exclusivity period for the small business debtor is 180 days, not 120 days for other debtors. Section 1121(e)(1) The debtor must file the disclosure statement and plan within 300 days of the petition. Section 1121(e)(2) These deadlines may be extended only on a showing that "it is more likely than not that the court will confirm a plan within a reasonable amount of time." Section 1121(e)(3)

3.6 The Plan Confirmation Procedure[233]

The plan and the disclosure statement can be the same document. Section 1125(f)(1) The disclosure statement may be "conditionally approved" and the hearing on the adequacy of the disclosure statement and confirmation of the plan can be combined. The court must confirm or deny the plan within 45 days after the plan is filed unless that deadline is extended by the court. Section 1129(e)

---

[233] Rule 3017.1 deals specifically with the procedure in small business cases. In the Central District, see Local Rule 3017-2. Final approval of the disclosure statement is required only when an objection is filed.

42.   SINGLE ASSET CASES

1.   General

A single asset chapter 11 case is one in which the debtor owns a single piece of real estate, other than residential property with fewer than four units, which property generates substantially all of the gross income of the estate. Section 101(51B)

2.   Duty to Make Mortgage Payments During the Case or File a Plan of Reorganization

The debtor must file a plan within 90 days "that has a reasonable possibility of being confirmed within a reasonable time." Section 362(d)(3) If the debtor does not file a plan, it must begin making monthly payments of an amount "equal to the interest at the then applicable non-default contract rate on the value of the creditor's interest in the real estate." If neither is done, the court must grant relief from stay to allow the creditor to begin or continue its foreclosure.

This requirement appears to be the only consequence of being designated a single asset case.   The term "single asset case" is not used anywhere else in the bankruptcy code and does not appear anywhere in the bankruptcy rules.

3.   Practical Problems Confirming a Plan in Single Asset Chapter 11 Cases

Debtors in single asset cases often have no significant debts other than the secured creditor which caused the filing in the first place. This creates the problem of getting a "consenting class" to vote for the plan. Section 1129(a)(10) If the debtor's property is worth less than the secured debt, the lien can be stripped down to the value of the property but the unsecured portion of the secured claim is grouped with the other unsecured creditors and is typically more than the total other unsecured debts. That means that the secured creditor controls both the secured class and the unsecured class and a no vote in both classes means the debtor does not have a consenting class.

If there is more than one secured creditor, in other words, more than one secured class, the task is a little easier. The debtor must offer good enough terms to get one of the secured creditors to vote for the plan although this often raises the issue of discrimination between the classes.

If the property is worth more than the liens, the secured creditor or creditors must be paid in full. The confirmation issues are the amount of interest, the term of the loan, feasibility and the absolute priority rule.

43.   POST CONFIRMATION MATTERS

1.   General

Confirmation of a Plan of Reorganization does not automatically end the chapter 11 proceeding although it is all but over for practical purposes. The Reorganized Debtor takes the property of the estate and commences its operations without the interference of the court or the prepetition creditors. Section 1141(b)

2.   Post-Confirmation Claims Litigation

Post-confirmation claims litigation is common in chapter 11 cases. The debtor may object to the amount or status of a claim and litigate the issue after the Plan has been confirmed. Some judges in the Central District will not confirm a Plan until all claims litigation has been completed.

3.   Final Fee Applications

Once the Plan has been confirmed, the court will set a date to hear final fee applications of the professionals in the case. This will include the debtor's counsel, the committee's counsel and accountants.

4.   The Final Decree

Once there are no further motions contemplated and all litigation has been completed and the Plan has been "substantially consummated," the debtor will file a Motion For a Final Decree.[234] Section 350   The granting of this motion formally ends the chapter 11 case. Substantially consummated generally means that the debtor has either commenced making payments called for under the Plan or has distributed property or has taken some action which cannot be undone.

44.   CHAPTER 11 COMPREHENSIVE EXAMPLES

1. Comprehensive Example One

222 Haskell, L.L.C. is owned 50% by Larry and 50% by Sherry. It owns a commercial building which the owners value at $2 million. Bank has a first mortgage of $1 million. Unsecured creditors total only $15,000. Larry is owed $100,000 for unsecured loans he has made to the debtor. Bank's loan has come due and it is threatening foreclosure.

1.1 Analysis

1.1.1 Valuation of the Building

Everything that happens in this case will depend heavily on the value of the building. It should be appraised early in the case. A separate hearing may even be required to ask the court to fix the value.

1.1.2 Cash Collateral

Bank has a lien on the rent generated by the building. This lien is standard in trust deed forms. Therefore, the debtor may not spend the rents received post-petition without the approval of the Bank or the court. Since Bank is adequately protected by the equity cushion, the court would allow the debtor to use the rent to pay the mortgage and pay the day to day expenses. The remainder would have to be sequestered.

---

[234] Rule 3022   *In re Ground Systems, Inc.*, 213 B.R. 1016 (B.A.P. 9th Cir. 1997) (setting forth factors)

1.1.3 The Plan

As to secured creditors, the debtor must pay the allowed secured claim of Bank in full with reasonable interest for a reasonable amount of time. Since Bank is heavily oversecured, low interest would be appropriate, amortized over 25 to 30 years with a balloon due in three to seven years. The unsecured creditors would have to be paid in full since the owners are going to retain their interest in the L.L.C. Larry's loan would not have to be paid in full since he, presumably, would vote for the plan. The only real problem that the debtor would have getting a plan confirmed over the objection of the Bank is getting one unimpaired, non-insider class to vote for the plan. There are only two classes here, Bank and unsecured creditors. Since, the unsecured creditors will be paid in full their vote does not count as one consenting class.

1.1.4 Conclusion

Assuming that the value of the building is really $2 million, it would be very unusual for this case to result in a bankruptcy petition being filed. It would be much cheaper for Larry and Sherry to refinance the building than to pay the cost of a chapter 11 proceeding. Also, since it is so likely that the Bank would be crammed down if reasonable interest were offered, assuming they have a consenting class, i.e., another secured creditor, it would likely agree to some sort of extension on the loan before forcing the bankruptcy filing.

2. Comprehensive Example Two

Assume the same facts as Example One except that the bank is owed $2.5 million.

2.1 Analysis

2.1.1 Cash Collateral

The court will be much more concerned about allowing the debtor to use the rent to pay the day to day expenses. Any use of cash collateral without the approval of Bank will be very limited in scope and very short term.

2.1.2 The Plan

Bank's secured claim is $2 million, the value of the building. It also has an unsecured claim of $500,000. As to secured creditors, the debtor must pay the $2 million secured claim of Bank in full with reasonable interest for a reasonable amount of time. Since there is no equity, interest would be higher, amortized over 25 to 30 years with a balloon due in no more than a few years. The unsecured creditors would have to be paid in full since the owners are going to retain their interest in the L.L.C. The unsecured class now includes the Bank. Its vote would control that class. The debtor has to get one unimpaired, non-insider class to vote for the plan. There are still only two classes here, Bank and unsecured creditors.

2.1.3 Conclusion

These cases were common in the early 1990s. It is very, very difficult to get a plan confirmed under these circumstances. In fact, the only way to save this building over the objection of Bank is for the owners to contribute significant funds as New Value and pay Bank in full, even the unsecured portion.

3. Comprehensive Example Three

Assume the building in Example One is owned by Larry and is his residence.

3.1 Analysis

3.1.1 Cash Collateral

There are no cash collateral issues as no rent is being paid to the debtor.

3.1.2 The Plan

Bank's secured claim must be paid in full according to its original terms. If the debtor is not able to do that, a plan cannot be confirmed over the objection of the Bank.

4. Comprehensive Example Four

Assume the debtor is a California corporation which owns a restaurant. Its balance sheet on the petition date, with assets at fair market value, is as follows:

Assets	F.M.V.	Liabilities	Amount
Cash	$ 5,000	Unsecured Creditors	$300,000
Inventory	10,000	IRS (payroll taxes)	100,000
Equipment	80,000	Loan from Owner	200,000
Liquor License	40,000		
Supplies	10,000	Common stock	10,000
Goodwill	50,000	Retained Earnings	(415,000)
Total	$195,000	Total	$195,000

4.1 Analysis

4.1.1 Cash Collateral

The initial inquiry must be whether or not the IRS is secured. If it is, the debtor may not spend or use the cash or inventory without the permission of the court. The court would probably allow the use of cash collateral without any problem since the IRS, a priority creditor, will get paid in full out of the remainder of the assets anyway and is therefore adequately protected.

4.1.2 The Restaurant Lease

The debtor does not own the building where the restaurant is operated and therefore it must lease it. Since the lease is for non-residential property, it must be assumed or rejected within 60 days after the case is filed. If the lease is assumed, the debtor must cure all defaults and offer assurance of its ability to perform in the future.

4.1.3 Asset Valuation

The typical chapter 11 case revolves around the value of the debtor's assets. In this case, an appraiser probably should be retained to give the debtor a professional opinion about the value of the assets.

4.1.4 The Plan

The plan must pay the creditors at least $195,000 since that is the amount they would receive in a liquidation. Of that amount, the IRS must be paid in full, since it is either secured or is a priority debt. Section 507. The IRS may be paid over a five year period. The plan, then could offer to pay the IRS approximately $3,770 per month for five years which would pay it in full with 6% interest. The plan could propose to pay the unsecured creditors, without the insiders, $100,000 (33% of their claims) over 48 months without interest or about $2,100 per month. Assuming that the unsecured creditors voted for the plan, it would be confirmed if the court found that the payments of $5,870 for 48 months and $3,770 for 36 months after that is feasible. This might be difficult since the debtor has apparently been losing money for some time. In any event, if the unsecured creditors vote against the plan, it will not be confirmed because it violates the absolute priority rule. The unsecured creditors would probably demand higher payments or a shorter time period in exchange for their accepting votes.

5. Comprehensive Example Five

Assume the same facts as example four except that the $200,000 loan from owner is a loan from bank, secured by a blanket lien on all assets of the estate.

5.1 Analysis

5.1.1 Cash Collateral

The cash collateral totals $15,000; i.e., $5,000 of cash and $10,000 of inventory. The debtor must adequately protect the bank's interest in these assets. A replacement lien in all post-petition cash and inventory, at least up to $15,000, would probably adequately protect the bank.

5.1.2 The Plan

The first and foremost problem here is the bank. It must be paid the amount of its secured claim, i.e., $200,000 in full with reasonable interest for a reasonable amount of time. Reasonable time is measured against the life of the collateral. Here, reasonable time is probably not more than a few years. Using 5 years and 9% interest, monthly payments would be $4,048. Since the debtor also has to pay the IRS in full, or $3,770 per month, it is going to need significant post-petition income or an investment from somewhere to have a chance getting a plan confirmed. In addition, the unsecured creditors are not going to wind up with much which means there is little to motivate them to vote for any plan. If they vote no, any plan will be rejected because of the absolute priority rule. A proposal of payments totaling $60,000 over 5 years or $1,000 per month is minimal. The total payments then is $8,818 for 5 years and $3,770 for one year after that. The debtor will have a difficult time establishing feasibility unless the business has suddenly become very profitable.

5.1.3 Conclusion

The bank will probably push hard for a shorter payoff than 5 years and higher interest than 9% unless it receives some additional collateral from the debtor's owners. The IRS will probably not get involved unless it really believes that the plan is not feasible. The IRS will certainly begin proceedings to assess the owners and begin trying to collect from them as well as receive payments under the plan. The unsecured creditors generally do not get too involved in these small cases. The few who vote at all would probably vote for the plan.

6. Comprehensive Example Six

Assume the debtor is a California corporation which owns a manufacturing business. Its balance sheet on the petition date, with assets at fair market value, is as follows:

Assets	F.M.V.	Liabilities	Amount
Cash	$ 50,000	Unsecured Creditors	$1,000,000
Inventory	650,000	IRS (payroll taxes)	100,000
Accounts Receivable	1,000,000	Bank Loan	2,000,000
Equipment	1,800,000	Loan from Owners	1,500,000
Supplies	10,000	Common stock	10,000
Catalogues	50,000	Retained Earnings	(1,050,000)
Total	$3,560,000	Total	$3,560,000

Sales are approximately $500,000 per month. The debtor employs 150 persons. It leases a large building but is two months behind on the rent. The bank has a security interest in cash, accounts receivable and inventory. The remainder of the assets are unencumbered.

6.1 Analysis

6.1.1 Cash Collateral

Cash collateral is a problem for this debtor. The bank is undersecured. It may want a liquidation and take what it can get rather than risk further deterioration of the assets of the debtor. The debtor will offer a replacement lien in postpetition assets which may improperly improve the position of the bank which is now unsecured.

6.1.2 The Building Lease

The debtor must assume the building lease or find someplace to move quickly. The lessor is going to demand that the past due rent be paid immediately. The bank however is not going to be too happy about allowing the debtor to use its cash collateral to pay the past due rent.

6.1.3 Asset Valuation

In this case, an appraiser probably should be retained to give the debtor a professional opinion about the value of the assets. In a liquidation, the equipment may sell for anywhere from 5% to 70% or 80% of its going concern value. This is going to be important in plan negotiations.

6.1.4 The Plan

The key player in this case is the bank. It must be paid $1,700,000, its allowed secured claim, with reasonable interest for a reasonable amount of time. Since the collateral has a short life, the stretch out period will not be long – a few years at most. Also, since it is, in effect, a 100% loan, with short term collateral, the interest rate will be substantial. How is the debtor going to make the payments, i.e., is any plan going to be feasible?

Assuming that the debtor can get the bank to go along with a plan, the unsecured creditors are going to have to be paid in full because they, apparently, would be paid in full in a liquidation. The IRS will have to be paid in full with interest over five years.

6.1.5 Conclusion

Unless the owners can put in significant new cash or the bank will go along with a long stretch out payment plan, the debtor is probably going to have to sell the business. It is highly unlikely that the business can generate enough cash to pay a plan over the objection of creditors. The creditors will see that a sale of the business will result in a large payment immediately and are unlikely to agree to a long stretch out period as well.

3284175

Made in the USA